America

A HISTORY OF THE
FIRST 500 YEARS

JOHN GRAFTON

PREFACE BY
James A. Michener

INTRODUCTION BY
Henry Steele Commager
WITH MARY COMMAGER

CRESCENT BOOKS
New York / Avinel, New Jersey

For my parents,
Edith and Samuel Grafton

This 1992 edition published by Crescent Books,
distributed by Outlet Book Company, Inc.
A Random House Company,
40 Engelhard Avenue,
Avinel, New Jersey 07001

A Rob Fremont Book

Picture Research: Carol Belanger Grafton
Associate Editors: Pati Cockram, Susan Martin, Sharon Smith
Assistant Editor: Sebnem Tokcan

Design by Carol Belanger Grafton
Composition: Trufont Typographers, Inc.

ACKNOWLEDGEMENTS

The editors would like to thank The Bettmann Archive, its director, David
Greenstein, and Katherine G. Bang especially, for their unique contribu-
tion to *America: A History of The First 500 Years*.

PRINTED AND BOUND IN HONG KONG BY LEEFUNG-ASCO PRINTERS

Library of Congress Cataloging-in-Publication Data

Grafton, John W., 1944–
    America : a history of the first 500 years / John W. Grafton, preface by James
Michener, introduction by Henry Steele Commager with Mary Commager.
        p.   cm.
    ISBN 0-517-06681-5
    1. United States—History—Pictorial works.   2. United States—History—
Chronology.   I. Michener, James A. (James Albert), 1907–.   II. Commager, Henry
Steele, 1902–   .   III. Title.
E178.5.G73   1992   91-35553
973—dc20   CIP

8 7 6 5 4 3 2 1

Preface

JAMES A. MICHENER

AMERICA IS A FORTUNATE COMBINATION of three magnificent assets: a continental landmass rich in mountains, rivers, minerals and much of the finest agricultural land in the world; an exciting mix of resilient people; and an idea of incandescent appeal, that a free people can govern themselves in all aspects of life. Nowhere else have these three components come together so fortuitously. We are a unique country.

I think we too often forget how fortunate we are in occupying the particular land we do. It is protected east and west by the world's two greatest oceans. Through the grace of a benevolent history we have good neighbors north and south and therefore peaceful boundaries. We are blessed with a life-giving complex of river systems. I never forget that the major difference between Australia and us, two nations of approximately the same size and form, is that Australia lacks a central river system, which leaves that vast segment of its land a near-desert, while we have that interlocking system of great rivers all feeding into the Mississippi. If a mighty hand could reach down and rip out that family of rivers, Illinois and Indiana, Iowa and Arkansas would also be near-desert.

America is also large enough to have accumulated by the chances of nature and geologic evolution concentrations of valuable ores, coal, oil and nutrients—a wealth of incalculable magnitude which has given our people the freedom to experiment in mining, manufacturing, agriculture and other economic adventures. Anyone surveying our prospects would be justified in concluding: this stretch of land was destined to be the base for a great nation, and even though we have sometimes abused our richness or used it to less than capacity, we have not yet destroyed it. Here it waits for our utilization and development.

We have been fortunate in having been founded ten or twenty thousand years ago by extremely brave forebears who had the courage to explore into this continent from their home base in Siberia and other portions of eastern Asia. Here they established patterns of land use, traditions for utilizing the terrain intelligently, and the establishment of a society that functioned remarkably well, though at a less rapid speed than those in Asia and Europe. Our Indians gave us a heritage of which they and we can be proud.

Spectacular were the accomplishments of the European adventurers when they arrived, for they brought with them the seeds of an advanced civilization. As one who has lived in the western part of our nation and worked in its historical materials, I am always mindful that Hispanic people arrived in what is now the United States a century before the English arrived in their Virginia and Massachusetts, and that the French had trading settlements along the Mississippi River systems long before any Englishmen arrived in those parts.

But the various intellectual and spiritual systems that the English brought with them—religion, law, finance, education—determined the early character of our nation, and we were fortunate that we started with strong bases from which to grow. Also, when blacks arrived they tended to be some of the ablest and best that Africa produced. And those who immigrated later were, as Professor Commager will amply prove, the daring, the adventurous and the survivors of their parent societies. A Chinese who came to this country to help build our railroads across the continent, operate our mines in Colorado and California, or help catch our salmon in Alaska had to be a person of daring, the kind of man or woman needed to build a strong nation.

I believe that a Scandinavian who settled in nineteenth century Minnesota or Dakota, or a peon from El Salvador who makes the perilous trip north in 1992 demonstrates the same determination that the English settlers showed in 1607 in Virginia and 1619 in Massachusetts. How lucky we were to have received such nation-builders.

This book pays tribute to the human actors in our vivid history. It cannot show the richness of the land of which I spoke, nor depict the third component of our greatness which I deem so important to our national life: the world of ideas. I wish to stress this conclusion garnered from a lifetime of studying and visiting all parts of our nation: I do not believe our incoming people, even though they were of fine character, could have used our national richness to build a nation unless they were guided and reinforced by a body of beliefs that sustained them through droughts, battles, economic depressions, and other temporary setbacks. They believed in freedom, in the individual worth of each woman or man, in the educability of children, in the ability of citizens to govern themselves without kings or an inherited noble class, and in the free exchange of ideas in the constant battle for the mind.

And through the long refinements of human aspirations from the earliest civilizations, through the speculations of the Greeks, the religious contributions of the Hebrews and later the Christians, and the probings of our philosophers and psychologists, our people brought with them and cultivated on these shores a moral and spiritual body of beliefs that have been called alternatively religion, or ethics, or a moral code, or divine guidance. However defined, however practiced, this body of beliefs, this search for the decent life, has been the foundation of our law, our government and our education of new generations. When we have strayed too far from that core belief we have done so at our peril.

What a magnificent nation we have received from our ancestors. What a noble task we face in passing it along to following generations in a strong and healthful condition.

JAMES A. MICHENER
Texas Center for Writers
Austin, Texas

Table of Contents

Introduction   vii

Chronology   ix

The Spanish Century   1

Christopher Columbus / Amerigo Vespucci / Francisco Vásquez de Coronado / Juan Ponce de León / Hernando de Soto / Giovanni da Verrazano / Sir Francis Drake

The English Colonies   5

Pocahontas / The Pilgrims / The First Thanksgiving / Henry Hudson / Peter Minuit / William Penn / Jacques Marquette / René Robert Cavelier, sieur de La Salle / Salem Witch Trials / Harvard College / Louis Hennepin

Toward Independence   11

French and Indian War / Daniel Boone / Boston Tea Party / Boston Massacre / Bunker Hill / Lexington and Concord / Patrick Henry / Declaration of Independence / Washington Crossing the Delaware / Nathan Hale / Valley Forge / Yorktown / Signing of the Constitution / George Washington / Thomas Jefferson / John Adams

Growth of a Nation 23

Eli Whitney / Sacajawea / War of 1812 / Edgar Allan Poe / Erie Canal / The Alamo / Samuel F.B. Morse / Stephen Foster / California Gold Rush / Sojourner Truth / John Brown / Pony Express / Abraham Lincoln / Bull Run / Battle of Gettysburg / Appomattox / John Wilkes Booth / Louisa May Alcott / First Transcontinental Railroad / Chicago Fire / Alexander Graham Bell / Statue of Liberty / Sitting Bull / Brooklyn Bridge / Mark Twain / Geronimo / Wounded Knee / Spanish-American War / Susan B. Anthony

The American Century 63

Immigration / Wright Brothers / Helen Keller / San Francisco Earthquake / Jack Johnson / Ty Cobb / Ford Motor Co. / Titanic / Margaret Sanger / John D. Rockefeller, Sr. / D. W. Griffith / World War I / Irving Berlin / George Gershwin / Clarence Darrow / Marian Anderson / Charles A. Lindbergh / The Depression / Shirley Temple / Franklin Delano Roosevelt / Hindenburg / Joe Louis / World War II / Louis Armstrong / Korean War / Elvis Presley / Marilyn Monroe / John Fitzgerald Kennedy / Martin Luther King, Jr. / Vietnam / Watergate / Ronald Reagan / Desert Storm / H. Norman Schwarzkopf

Picture Index 131

Introduction

HENRY STEELE COMMAGER
WITH MARY COMMAGER

For nearly five centuries the very word America has fired the world's imagination and longing. Almost since Columbus's triumphant return to Barcelona in 1493, peoples everywhere—the disinherited and the dispossessed—who dreamed of adventure, of a haven and a refuge, of an opportunity for wealth and liberty, looked to America. And for countless immigrants over the centuries such dreams became reality on her shores.

For some, mostly from Europe, the transformation came quickly and dramatically. For others, particularly those descended from Africans forced to migrate as slaves, slowly; for slavery did not end until 1865 and it took another one hundred years for the promises of Abraham Lincoln to be kept. And for those eking out their existence today in the urban slums of New York or Chicago, Los Angeles or Washington, the dream appears all but dead. Yet, America, even an America where racism and poverty tarnish its image at home and materialism and imperialism tarnish its image abroad, continues to shine globally as a beacon to a brighter future, to economic opportunity, and to political freedom.

At first it was South America and the very existence of a "New World" largely unexplored that excited the "Old World" of Europe. Columbus, sailing under charter to Spain's Isabella, and others who followed quickly in his wake, brought back incredible tales of new flora and fauna, new riches to mine, new souls to harvest. Mapmakers hastened to correct their old vision of the world; the printing press, which provoked a fifteenth century revolution in communication unmatched until the computer in the twentieth century, spread both the sailors' tales and the new maps quickly. And one seafaring publicist, the Italian Amerigo Vespucci, whose famous *Mundus Novus* was read throughout Europe, earned immortality when the German cartographer Waldseemüller affixed his name to the new found lands.

As the stories spread, as disbelief faded, scholars came to debate the importance of the startling discovery. How could it be? Where had this land been all these centuries? Whence came its people, strange of color and customs? Did they have souls? Were they the descendants of a long forgotten settlement of Egyptians or Ethiopians, or of shipwrecked Phoenicians, or a Lost Tribe of Israel?

While the scholars debated, soldiers and sailors continued to set out from Spain. Further explorations revealed fabulous cities, great civilizations, vast empires. The conquistadors themselves stood in awe of what they saw—and were about to destroy. For it went beyond the bounds of their experience and imagination, as the irascible old Bernal Díaz del Castillo, who marched with Hernando Cortés, tells us:

> *It was all so wonderful that I do not know how to describe the first glimpse of things never heard of, seen or dreamed of before.*

Cortés's conquest of Mexico and Pizarro's conquest of Peru made Spain a world power and the envy of all Europe. And the nations of all Europe hastened to lay claim to their own New World empires by sending out explorers and settlers. Busily the monarchs of France, England and the Netherlands plotted and promoted expeditions. True, in 1494 Pope Alexander VI had drawn a line down the middle of the still uncharted new world and given to the Spanish and the Portuguese the right to conquer and colonize and Christianize Columbus's "guile-

less and unwarlike savages," his "Indians." But the rest of Europe agreed not with the Pope. Why should they? As France's Francois I bluntly declared, nowhere did there exist "a clause in the last will of Adam conceding such exclusive control to Kings Manoel and Charles."

In the seventeenth and eighteenth centuries the English would prove to be the great colonizers of North America, founding colonies up and down the coast. Thus, it is to England that the United States owes its largest debt for those political principles and institutions that are America's greatest achievement, and which, along with the belief in a divinely inspired destiny and the bounty of a limitless frontier, were all that held the young nation together after 1776.

It has been an enduring achievement. America is, after all, of the major countries active on the world's stage, the oldest republic, the oldest democracy, the oldest federal system; it has the oldest written constitution and boasts the oldest—for good or bad—of genuine political parties, political parties which cut across class lines and lines drawn by religion and culture and language, and gave diverse people a voice in the new country.

If America no longer holds as a model for others to imitate unquestioningly, it remains an inspiration for those who aspire to democracy. For Americans invented the constitutional convention and created a government that, no matter how imperfect the results, set out to resolve the most perplexing problems—how to reconcile liberty and order, localism and centralization, church and state, political democracy and economic inequality—and set out to accomplish all of this without benefit of the unifying forces of religion or a royal house.

The Founders of the American Republic proved to be men of wisdom as well as learning. Trained as most of them were in the history of Greece and Rome, steeped in the new science of the Enlightenment from France and England, they set out to base their country on that history and on that science. They created a nation based on the principles of the classical philosophers; that is, on the principles of republicanism. The Public Thing—*res publica*—was the basis of their political philosophy and they made that philosophy a working reality. They incorporated the writings of Englishmen like John Locke and that stellar assembly of France's *philosophes*, who promoted the rights of man over the rights of monarchs, into their documents of creation.

By great good fortune, the new United States started with the leadership of men like George Washington and Thomas Jefferson, John Adams and Alexander Hamilton, James Madison and John Jay; a leadership which was incomparable in the eighteenth century and has remained incomparable to the present day. This galaxy of leaders was not to be matched, even by those who led later democratic revolutions in France or in Germany or in the other countries of the Old World and the New. How this happened is almost inexplicable, for America at the time boasted no great centers of learning; it provided its citizens with no effective practice in the daily conduct of nations. Yet somehow they managed and managed well, commanding the respect of their fellow citizens at the time and the respect and admiration of their descendants today. Consider but one example: three young men, Hamilton, Madison and Jay sat down and in a matter of weeks wrote a political masterpiece, *The Federalist Papers*, still read and studied today in every civilized country. Could all the assembled wisdom of our great graduate schools of Political Science equal that achievement today?

Whatever its modern flaws, how extraordinary that this new nation with a total population of only some 3 million was able to set standards for much of the world and has continued to do so, in one way or another, to the present day. For many at the time gave it little hope. Few outside of America believed as did England's Horace Walpole, writing to Sir Horace Mann in 1774, that

The next Augustine Age will dawn on the other side of the Atlantic. There will perhaps be a Thucydides at Boston, a Xenophon at New York.

Democracy was an ideal, to be sure, but one that had seen little practical application. And the Founders managed to create an entire nation that was indeed democratic at the federal level, as well as in town meetings and in state politics. Thirteen states came to be a self-sufficient nation, a working federal republic. Their wisdom is reflected in the Constitution, a document which has proven flexible enough to survive the changes wrought by America's conversion to a manufacturing country, its emergence as a world power, its loss of that marvelous "Equality of Condition," noted by foreign observers like Alexis de Tocqueville as essential to the success of America.

In order to accomplish this, the Founders did what had not been done before: they created a new kind of nationalism. It was a nationalism without a king or common religion or culture. It was a nationalism that came to rest on political institutions, on the principle of government by the people—and a people that would come eventually from every corner of the globe. We take that for granted. But it was taken for granted in few European or American countries then or now. Quite the contrary!

No nation in Europe proved as effective politically as did the new American nation based as it was on democracy, a nation made by the people, concerned above all else with *res publica*, the public thing or public welfare. That concern soon caught on in one European nation after another and worldwide, but it was the Americans who set the example, even in France and Germany. And the Americans who set the example, too, of creating a single state out of thirteen quasi independent states and creating one people out of emigrants from all around the world. No easy feat that last. For peoples of many cultures, of many languages and religions had not in the past proved a solid basis for independent nations.

Yet almost from the country's beginnings, a steady stream of peoples, of all colors and cultures and faiths, came to swell the population of the new nation. To be sure, the English predominated in the early settlements, but soon they were joined and intermingled with the Scots and Scots-Irish, the Dutch, the Swedes, the French Huguenots, the Germans, and the Africans. Together they comprised the colonial population.

Throughout the nineteenth and twentieth centuries new Americans arrived. Not all peoples, to be sure, entered the country willingly. Not all had to cross an ocean to become part of the American republic. Expansion forced many, in the years following Independence, to come under the flag—the benefits of the Constitution following all too slowly. Thus Seminoles and Navajos, Cherokees and Comanches, French and Spanish and Mexican residents of Louisiana, Florida, Texas and California came to live in American territory as part of the conquest of a continent.

Most, however, embraced America willingly. They were those Emma Lazarus sought to immortalize in her eloquent entreaty engraved on the base of the Statue of Liberty:

Give me your tired, your poor,
Your huddled masses yearning to breathe free,
The wretched refuse of your teeming shore,
Send these, the homeless, tempest-tossed to me . . .

As long as famine and draught, war and persecution for faith or creed pushed people from their homelands, America's promise of greater freedom and opportunity continued to pull them here. Irish, Germans, Scandinavians, Italians, Poles, Russians, Chinese, and Japanese all came and together formed the American nation.

True, the United States, to its discredit, has often reacted to newcomers with suspicion, even imposing quotas on immigration, but no legislation has ever stemmed the tide completely. Today, with a population of some 250 million,

immigration continues. Most recently large numbers come from the other American countries—from Cuba and Mexico, from Haiti and the Dominican Republic; and from Southeast Asia—from Vietnam and Cambodia, Thailand and Korea.

All these came, and continue to come to America, bringing their dreams and their desire, whatever their differences, to blend together to become Americans. For so it has happened. Americans have built upon their European and African, Asian and Latin inheritance something that is rooted clearly in western civilization, yet remains unique. Photographic collections such as this book make clear the contributions of all that came, the wonderful diversity of the American social scene—the mixtures of races and people, cultures and religions—which vindicate the national motto: "E pluribus unum."

The institutions and ideas that have made this possible, no matter how slowly or imperfectly, did not grow in a vacuum. They were not mere duplication of Europe, certainly not of England. One need only look at the varied results of transplanting British institutions to Canada, Australia, South Africa and Jamaica to recognize that truth. Differences evolved not only because of social diversity but because of a different environment, of the demands of a frontier, and of a history that was itself, partly the result of that frontier and environment.

While grand civilizations existed long before Europe's intrusion into America, in the eyes and minds of those who emigrated from the Old World, America seemed spacious and empty. It beckoned with the promise of land, a wild land awaiting the taming of civilization as developed in Europe. For much of our history, it has been this very vastness, this image of a new land awaiting new people that has contributed to America's uniqueness.

And so in spite of the broken dreams of many, of the despair and death that awaited some in the distant Promised Land, America proved all that could be hoped for to others, whether they clung to the Atlantic and Pacific coasts in the first centuries of colonization or moved, as the country moved, into the interior in succeeding waves.

Our modern eyes look with disfavor on the wanton destruction of Amerindian civilization; and on the destruction, too, of what had once seemed a boundless and bountiful nature that would provide in Jefferson's felicitous phrase for "our descendants to the thousandth and thousandth generation." We point accusingly and with justice to the crimes committed by those who sought to fulfill America's manifest destiny. We despair that America falls so short of its promises to so many.

We must remember to look not only at destruction but at creation. Lacking a common culture and religion, Americans had to invent a nation where there was none. It is because those of another generation were successful at doing so that we can now step back and criticize freely what took place before. And if we are willing—and do not waste our energies on petty squabbles—we can build still on the foundations which have endured.

Thus, we return to the success of America in the arena of politics. For this above all has been the great achievement of America, to fashion a republic that endured. Surely not perfect, surely not without compelling blemishes, but nevertheless a remarkable achievement when contrasted with the faltering steps towards democracy taken elsewhere. For some two hundred years the American republic has stood as a symbol to the powerless, to the disinherited, to the disenfranchised everywhere. Slow as it has been to provide for equality, to open the doors to political participation, it continues to move forward towards that noble ideal of government of the people, by the people, and for the people. And it remains the people, no matter when or whence they came originally, who hold the responsibility for America's continued success. George Washington's words remain as true today as when he penned them in 1789 for his First Inaugural:

The preservation of the sacred fire of liberty, and the destiny of the republican model of government, are justly considered as deeply, perhaps as finally staked, on the experiment entrusted to the hands of the American people.

HENRY STEEL COMMAGER
MARY COMMAGER
Amherst, Massachusetts
August, 1991

Chronology

1492 On October 12 at 2:00 A.M., the *Pinta*, one of Christopher Columbus's three ships, fires shot to signal her sighting of an island.

1507 Mapmaker Martin Waldseemüller labels the recently discovered land "America" after navigator Amerigo Vespucci.

1513 Vasco Nuñez de Balboa sights the body of water known as the Pacific "peaceful" ocean.

1513 Juan Ponce de León, in search of the Fountain of Youth, encounters land mass he calls Florida.

1524 New York bay and Hudson River are sighted by Italian explorer Giovanni da Verrazano.

1540 Grand Canyon and Colorado River are sighted and named by Spanish explorer under Coronado, García López de Cárdenas, while seeking the Seven Cities of Gold of Cibola.

1541 Mississippi River is encountered by Hernando de Soto and named Río del Espíritu Santo.

1543 Juan Rodriguez Cabrillo explores Pacific coast from southern California to Oregon, discovering San Diego and San Francisco bays.

1565 Saint Augustine, Spanish colony, becomes the oldest permanent city in North America.

1579 Captain Francis Drake, on first English expedition around the world, explores Pacific coastline of the Americas.

1584 Sir Walter Raleigh claims 1,800 miles of North American coastline for England; names land Virginia for "Virgin Queen," Elizabeth I.

1587 First child of European descent, Virginia Dare, is born in North America at the third colony at Roanoke.

1600 North American Plains tribes first acquire horses and guns from Spaniards.

1602 Captain Bartholomew Gosnold, first Englishman to come ashore in Northeast, explores and names Cape Cod and Martha's Vineyard.

1605 European diseases—smallpox, measles, dysentery, typhoid and tuberculosis—decimate native populations in North and South America; perhaps 90% of the Indians in New Spain die.

1607 Jamestown Colony, first permanent British settlement in North America, is established in Virginia.

1607 Captain John Smith of Jamestown is captured by Powhatan tribe and spared by efforts of chief's daughter, Pocahontas.

1609 English explorer Henry Hudson, seeking sea route to the Indies, sails up Hudson River.

1619 House of Burgesses, first assembly in New World, convenes in Jamestown.

1620 Pilgrims, 41 British families, land at Plymouth Rock and establish colony.

1621 First Thanksgiving feast is held at Plymouth to celebrate survival of first winter.

1626 Dutchman Peter Minuit buys Manhattan Island from the Indians for $24.

1634 Maryland is founded by George Calvert as Catholic colony.

1636 Harvard College is founded by Mass. Bay Colony puritans, named in 1639.

1664 Dutch surrender New Amsterdam. Renamed New York by British.

1676 King Philip's War is fought between New England Indians and colonists.

1682 René Robert Cavelier, sieur de La Salle sails down Mississippi River, naming territory Louisiana after Louis XIV.

1682 William Penn founds Quaker colony. Signs Indian peace treaty in 1683.

1689 France and Great Britain fight King William's War (–1697) for control of North American territories.

1704 Queen Anne's War, part of larger War of Spanish Succession, sees British win much of French colonial territory.

1733 James Oglethorpe founds Georgia colony with debtors.

1752 Benjamin Franklin publishes *Experiments and Observations on Electricity*.

1756 In French and Indian War (–1763), English defeat French, gain Canadian and eastern colonial territory. Spain, meanwhile, occupies West.

1765 British impose Stamp Act, a tax on publications, in colonial America. Opposition forces its repeal in 1766.

1767 Anti-British sentiment deepens after passage of Townshend Acts, a tax on imports.

1770 In Boston Massacre, civilians and troops clash in bloody riot.

1773 Colonials empty tea into Boston Harbor to protest British tea tax.

1775 Paul Revere rides to Concord to warn minutemen of impending British march to seize colonial arsenal. Battles of Lexington and Concord herald start of war.

1776 *Common Sense*, a widely distributed pamphlet by Thomas Paine, sells almost half a million copies and helps garner public support for Revolution.

1776 Continental Congress adopts and posts *Declaration of Independence*.

1777 Articles of Confederation, approved by Continental Congress, become law of the land in 1781 upon ratification.

1778 Hawaii (Sandwich Isl.) is discovered by Capt. James Cook.

1781 British surrender at Yorktown. U.S. sovereignty assured.

1788 Constitution takes effect when 9 of 13 states ratify it. The Bill of Rights is proposed (ratified 1791).

1789 George Washington is unanimously elected first President.

1792 New York Stock Exchange has first informal meeting under tree on Wall Street.

1792 New capital on the Potomac is designed by Pierre l'Enfant, completed in 1800.

1793 Eli Whitney invents the cotton gin.

1800 Thomas Jefferson is elected President by House of Representatives after electoral tie with Aaron Burr.

1801 War with Tripoli (–1805) begins over U.S. refusal to pay for protection of shipping interests.

1803 In landmark *Marbury* v. *Madison* case, U.S. Supreme Court first voids an act of Congress as unconstitutional.

1803 U.S. doubles its size with Louisiana Purchase by acquiring French territory in the Middle West for $15 million.

1804 Meriwether Lewis and William Clark explore Louisiana Purchase territory and the West to Pacific Ocean.

1807 Trading of slaves is outlawed by Great Britain and United States.

1807 Fulton launches steamboat *Clermont*.

1812 Conflicts over shipping and British impressment of American sailors lead to War of 1812. Toronto (1813) and Washington, D.C. (1814) are burned. Failed British attack of Baltimore's Fort McHenry inspires Francis Scott Key to write *The Star Spangled Banner*.

1819 Spain cedes Florida to U.S. in exchange for cancellation of debt and U.S. claims to Texas.

1820 "Legend of Sleepy Hollow" and "Rip Van Winkle" are published by Washington Irving, the first American to gain international literary fame.

1820 Missouri Compromise keeps delicate balance between free and slave states by admitting Missouri as slave state and Maine as free state.

1823 Monroe Doctrine bars further colonization of Western Hemisphere by European powers.

1825 Erie Canal, 363-mile-long waterway, links Middle West to the Hudson River Valley.

1826 The *Last of the Mohicans*, James Fenimore Cooper's classic novel, depicts early frontier.

1826 Jedediah Strong Smith becomes first to cross Southwest to California.

1830 Baltimore & Ohio Railroad demonstrates first steam-powered locomotive.

1833 Oberlin is first U.S. college to admit women.

1833 John Deere manufactures steel plow blades, formerly made of cast iron.

1834 Cyrus McCormick patents automatic grain-reaper.

1836 Alamo falls to Santa Anna in Texas fight for independence from Mexico. Within year, tide turns and Texas becomes republic; joins Union in 1845.

1838 Underground Railroad, which helps escaped slaves flee north, names Robert Purvis president.

1839 Charles Goodyear discovers process which vulcanizes rubber.

1841 "Murders in the Rue Morgue" is one of Edgar Allan Poe's many eerie but spellbinding works.

1842 Army Lt. John Charles Frémont explores Rocky Mountains and Wyoming with Kit Carson.

1843 Sewing machine is invented by Elias Howe.

1844 Samuel F. B. Morse sends first telegraph transmission: "What hath God wrought?"

1846 War between United States and Mexico over territorial dispute enables U.S. to acquire Southwest and California for $15 million.

1848 New York law allows married women to own real estate.

1848 First women's rights meeting under Elizabeth Cady Stanton and Lucretia Mott, holds that "all men and women are created equal."

1848 California gold rush begins.

1850 Nathaniel Hawthorne's *The Scarlet Letter* describes Puritan morals in 17th Century New England.

1852 Antislavery novel *Uncle Tom's Cabin* by Harriet Beecher Stowe sells 300,000 copies.

1854 In *Walden*, Henry David Thoreau meditates on the glory of nature.

1855 Henry Wadsworth Longfellow publishes *Hiawatha* (1855).

1855 The controversial *Leaves of Grass* is published by Walt Whitman.

1857 Supreme Court in Dred Scott case finds slavery inalienable right of all states and territories, voids Missouri Compromise as unconstitutional.

1859 First commercial oil well is drilled in Titusville, Pennsylvania.

1859 Harper's Ferry raid, attempt by abolitionist John Brown to seize arsenal in Virginia and start slave uprising, fails.

1860 Abraham Lincoln wins Presidential election despite South's dire warnings.

1860 South Carolina starts wave of secession among Cotton Belt states after Lincoln's election.

1861 Ft. Sumter is bombarded by Confederate troops, precipitating Civil War.

1863 Emancipation Proclamation is issued by Lincoln, freeing slaves.

1863 Over 1,200 die when New York City workers riot over draft law.

1865 Thirteenth Amendment to Constitution abolishes slavery in United States.

1865 Lee surrenders at Appomattox Courthouse after fall of Richmond (April 9).

1865 President Lincoln is shot and killed by John Wilkes Booth (April 15).

1867 United States buys Alaska from Russia for $7.2 million.

1868 In *Little Women*, Louisa May Alcott tells the enduring story of four sisters growing up in New England.

1869 Golden spike driven at Promontory, Utah completes the U.S. transcontinental railroad.

1869 Knights of Labor is founded. By 1886, it has 700,000 members and achieves some reforms.

1870 Standard Oil Company is incorporated by John D. Rockefeller. By 1880s he controls 80% of U.S. oil refining operations and 90% of U.S. oil pipelines.

1871 Great Chicago Fire leaves 100,000 homeless.

1876 Telephone is patented by Alexander Graham Bell.

1876 Col. George Custer and 262 troops are killed at Little Big Horn in territorial dispute with Sioux and Cheyenne Indians.

1877 Thomas A. Edison invents phonograph, electric light bulb (1879), Kinetoscope (1889).

1878 *Daisy Miller*, is published by novelist Henry James.

1879 George B. Seldon applies for horseless carriage patent.

1883 Brooklyn Bridge, longest in world (1,595 ft) at time, is completed.

1886 Statue of Liberty is unveiled in New York.

1889 Dow Jones begins publishing daily newspaper, *Wall Street Journal*.

1890 In *Poems*, Emily Dickinson is finally published four years after her death.

1890 Sherman Antitrust Act is passed, aimed at breaking up monopolies.

1890 153 Sioux Indians are slaughtered by U.S. cavalry at Wounded Knee Creek, South Dakota.

1891 U.S. Forest Reserve Act designates 13 million acres of land as reservations.

1892 Ellis Island, immigrant receiving station, opens to process half-million newcomers annually.

1892 Coca-Cola Co. is founded using 1886 Atlanta recipe.

1894 Hershey chocolate bar is invented in Pennsylvania.

1895 In *The Red Badge of Courage*, Stephen Crane presents a powerful view of the Civil War.

1896 Henry Ford builds his first car, a two-cylinder "quadricycle."

1897 Gold Rush in Klondike region begins.

1898 In Spanish-American War, United States gains control of Philippines, Cuba and Puerto Rico.

1898 Hawaii is annexed by U.S. after monarchy is overthrown.

1900 *The Wonderful Wizard of Oz*, L. Frank Baum's most enduring work, is published.

1900 Dr. Walter Reed discovers that malaria is transmitted by infected mosquitoes.

1900 Eastman Kodak introduces $1 Brownie camera, popularizing photography.

1901 Discovery of oil fields at Spindletop hints at Texas's vast deposits.

1901 Pres. McKinley is assassinated by anarchist; Theodore Roosevelt takes office.

1902 Brooklyn store owner develops and sells first "teddy bear" named after President Theodore Roosevelt.

1903 *The Call of the Wild*, Jack London's classic novel, tells of the rugged Alaska wilderness.

1903 Ford Motor Company opens in Detroit.

1903 Panama is recognized as an independent state after U.S.-backed rebellion paves way for construction of canal (opened in 1914).

1903 Movies advance from skits to narratives with the 12-minute film *The Great Train Robbery* by Edwin S. Porter.

1903 Boston defeats Pittsburgh 5–3 in first World Series.

1903 Wright Brothers achieve flight in heavier-than-air craft at Kitty Hawk.

1906 *The Jungle*, the classic muckraking novel by Upton Sinclair, paints an unforgiving picture of the Chicago meat-packing industry.

1906 San Francisco earthquake and subsequent fire destroy downtown district.

1906 Audion vacuum tube—essential to radio, television, telephone, radar—is invented and patented by Lee De Forest.

1908 Ford Motor Company introduces Model T.

1909 Robert Edwin Peary and Matthew Henson reach North Pole.

1909 Architect Frank Lloyd Wright builds the Robie House in "Prairie School" style.

1912 British liner *Titanic* collides with iceberg; 1,513 die on maiden voyage.

1913 Sixteenth Amendment to Constitution gives Congress power to impose income taxes.

1913 Ford improves assembly-line production of Model T, lowering its price.

1916 *Road Not Taken* garners acclaim for poet Robert Frost.

1916 Margaret Sanger opens first birth-control clinic in Brooklyn, N.Y.

1917 Germany's World War I (1914–18) submarine warfare against merchant shipping brings U.S. into war on Allied side (April 6).

1918 President Wilson's 14 Points, announced at Paris Peace Conference after World War I, include establishment of League of Nations, which U.S. later refuses to join.

1920 Nineteenth Amendment to Constitution gives women the right to vote.

1922 Teapot Dome scandal breaks, involving Harding administration's exchange of leases on federal oil lands for bribes.

1923 Henry Luce founds *Time* magazine; in 1936, *Life* magazine.

1924 Drawing on original jazz themes, George Gershwin composes *Rhapsody in Blue*.

1925 Clarence Darrow's brilliant defense of John Scopes for teaching evolution fails to save Scopes from conviction.

1925 Against the backdrop of the Roaring Twenties, F. Scott Fitzgerald depicts his American tragedy, *The Great Gatsby*.

1926 *Abraham Lincoln* by Carl Sandburg examines the classic American life.

1926 *The Sun Also Rises*, Ernest Hemingway's first novel, launches a fertile career rewarded in 1954 with the Nobel Prize for Literature.

1926 Scientist Robert H. Goddard fires liquid-fuel rocket into atmosphere, lays basis for modern rocketry.

1927 Talking motion pictures are ushered in with film *The Jazz Singer*.

1927 Charles Lindbergh makes first solo transatlantic flight, from New York to Paris, aboard *Spirit of St. Louis*.

1929 In *The Sound and the Fury*, William Faulkner, 1949 Nobel winner, explores the complex civilization of the American South.

1929 Stock-market crash catapults U.S. economy into Great Depression.

1930 Sinclair Lewis, author of *Main Street* (1920) and *Babbit* (1922), is awarded the Nobel Prize.

1930 First large-scale analog computer is built at MIT by Vannevar Bush.

1931 Physicist Ernest Lawrence invents cyclotron to accelerate atomic particles.

1931 Empire State Building (1,245 feet) is built; world's tallest for 43 years.

1931 Jane Addams, founder of Chicago's Hull House, is first woman to win Nobel Peace Prize.

1932 Amelia Earhart is first woman to fly solo across Atlantic; disappears in 1937 in round-the-world attempt.

1933 President Franklin Delano Roosevelt assumes first of four terms, promising a "New Deal."

1933 Solo round-the-world flight is completed by American Wiley Post in just under 8 days.

1933 Twenty-first Amendment to Constitution repeals prohibition.

1934 *Tropic of Cancer*, Arthur Miller's erotic masterpiece, causes controversy.

1934 U.S. Securities and Exchange Commission is established to prevent kinds of financial abuses that precipitated Stock Market Crash of 1929.

1935 Nylon, first synthetic fiber, is developed; nylon stockings available in 1938.

1935 American pilot Howard Hughes sets new world speed record of 352 mph.

1935 Social Security Act establishes unemployment compensation and pension benefits for workers.

1935 Labor leader John L. Lewis founds Committee for Industrial Organization (CIO).

1940 Richard Wright's novel *Native Son* makes him the first black author of a best-seller.

1941 FDR, having won unprecedented third term in 1940, outlaws discrimination in defense contracts and government employment.

1941 Regular television broadcasting begins with the licensing of NBC and CBS.

1941 In World War II (1939-45), U.S. neutrality ends with Japan's sneak attack on Pearl Harbor, December 7.

1942 FDR orders over 110,000 Japanese Americans interned in military camps.

1942 Italian-born American physicist Enrico Fermi and colleagues produce first sustained nuclear reaction, paving way for atomic bomb and nuclear energy development.

1944 Allied invasion of Normandy lands over 150,000 troops in France.

1945 First successful testing of American-made atomic bomb is conducted in New Mexico (July 16).

1945 United States drops atomic bombs on Hiroshima and later Nagasaki to compel Japanese to surrender (August).

1945 U.S. joins United Nations.

1947 *Tales of the South Pacific* launches James A. Michener's prolific career as a writer of novels that tell the American story.

1947 President Truman declares U.S. Cold War policy of containing spread of communism.

1947 Marshall Plan provides massive economic aid to war-torn Europe.

1947 Test pilot Charles E. (Chuck) Yeager breaks sound barrier in rocket plane.

1948 Norman Mailer's novel *The Naked and the Dead* establishes him as a conspicuous figure on the American literary scene.

1948 In Berlin Blockade, U.S. supplies West Berlin by airlift until Soviets end blockade in 1949.

1948 William Shockley and colleagues at Bell Labs invent the transistor.

1948 Armed forces are ordered integrated by President Truman.

1948 State Department official Alger Hiss is accused of spying for Soviet Union.

1949 In *Death of a Salesman*, playwright Arthur Miller examines the American dream, the family, the individual and society.

1949 United States joins North Atlantic Treaty Organization (NATO), a mutual defense alliance pact among eleven nations.

1950 Senator Joseph R. McCarthy begins hearings to root out and blacklist suspected Communist sympathizers in U.S. The Senate finally censures McCarthy in 1954.

1950 When North Korea crosses 38th parallel, U.S. provides military forces to help repel Communist invasion. By armistice in 1953, over 55,000 Americans are dead and over 100,000 wounded.

1950 Ralph Bunche, U.N. diplomat, is first black American to win Nobel Peace Prize, for his work mediating Middle East conflict.

1951 First nuclear reactor is built by U.S. Atomic Energy Commission. Electricity generated there is first used in 1955.

1952 First H-bomb, exploded by U.S. in Marshall Islands, is world's first thermonuclear device.

1952 Ralph Ellison publishes his novel of black experience, *The Invisible Man*, for which he wins the National Book Award.

1952 J.D. Salinger captures imagination of American youth in classic novel, *The Catcher in the Rye*.

1952 E.B. White enchants children and their parents with his beloved story, *Charlotte's Web*.

1953 U.S. biologist James Watson and British physicist Francis Crick describe double helix structure of DNA molecule.

1953 Julius and Ethel Rosenberg are executed for giving Soviets information on atomic bomb.

1953 James Baldwin's novel *Go Tell It on the Mountain* confirms him as a critical black American spokesman.

1954 First Lady Mamie Eisenhower christens *Nautilus*, world's first nuclear-powered submarine.

1954 Polio vaccine developed by Dr. Jonas Salk is licensed by government.

1954 In *Brown* v. *Board of Education* of Topeka, Kansas, Supreme Court denies validity of separate-but-equal public school facilities.

1955 Year-long bus boycott begins among Montgomery, Alabama blacks when Rosa Parks is arrested for refusing to sit in back of bus.

1957 With *On the Road*, Jack Kerouac establishes the Beat Generation's place in American literature.

1957 President Eisenhower orders National Guard to enforce Federal Court order desegregating Little Rock, Ark. Central High School.

1958 National Aeronautics and Space Administration (NASA) is created.

1958 First U.S. ICBM (intercontinental ballistic missile), Atlas, hits target in South Atlantic, 5,500 miles away.

1958 Launch of first U.S. man-made satellite, Explorer, follows Russia's Sputnik.

1958 Integrated circuit is invented by engineer Jack Kilby.

1959 Xerox introduces first copier.

1960 John Updike's *Rabbit Run* begins a series of novels that depict modern American life.

1960 FDA approves hormonal contraceptive pill.

1960 Nuclear sub *Triton* completes circumnavigation of globe without resurfacing, covering 41,500 miles in 84 days.

1960 Theodore Maimen develops first laser.

1960 Democrat John F. Kennedy is elected as youngest and first Catholic President by slim margin over Richard M. Nixon.

1961 Joseph Heller's irreverent novel, *Catch-22*, becomes an instant classic.

1961 Peace Corps is created by Kennedy to provide aid to developing nations.

1961 U.S. agrees to increase military advisors and aid to South Vietnam.

1961 Astronaut Alan B. Shepard, Jr. becomes first American in space.

1962 John Steinbeck is awarded the Nobel Prize after a lifetime of portraying the bitter side of life in such works as *The Grapes of Wrath* (1939).

1962 John H. Glenn Jr. orbits earth three times in spacecraft *Friendship 7* in first U.S. manned orbital flight.

1962 U.S. satellite Telstar 1 allows first transatlantic TV transmission.

1962 James Meredith, under protection of federal troops, becomes first black student at University of Mississippi amid riots that kill two.

1962 Khrushchev agrees to remove Russian missiles from Cuba after Kennedy threatens invasion.

1963 *Cat's Cradle* launches Kurt Vonnegut's literary career.

1963 Medgar Evers is assassinated.

1963 First successful minicomputer is developed by Digital Equipment Corporation.

1963 Martin Luther King, Jr. delivers "I have a dream" speech to 250,000 at Lincoln Memorial to urge passage of civil rights legislation.

1963 President John F. Kennedy is assassinated in Dallas.

1964 Civil Rights Act bans racial discrimination in public facilities and employment.

1964 Gulf of Tonkin incident leads to escalation of U.S. presence in Vietnam: 389,000 U.S. troops by 1966.

1965 Civil rights march from Selma to Montgomery, Ala. is marred by violence.

1965 Voting Rights Act bans poll taxes, literacy and other tests designed to limit minority voters.

1965 Riots in Watts section of Los Angeles in August cause 34 deaths and more than $40 million in property damage.

1966 In *Miranda* v. *Arizona*, U.S. Supreme Court overturns validity of confession because suspect was not told his rights.

1967 *The Confessions of Nat Turner* is published by William Styron. *Sophie's Choice* follows in 1979.

1967 Riots in Detroit and hundreds of other cities cause 100 deaths and more than $500 million damage.

1967 DNA is synthesized by Stanford University biochemists.

1968 Martin Luther King, Jr. is assassinated by James Earl Ray in Memphis, Tenn. (April 4), setting off riots in more than 40 cities.

1968 Senator Robert A. Kennedy is shot by Sirhan Sirhan in Los Angeles, (June 6) after winning California Democratic Presidential primary.

1969 *Apollo 11* mission lands first men on the moon. Astronauts Neil A. Armstrong and Edwin E. Aldrin, Jr. descend to Tranquillity Base in Lunar Module, the "Eagle." Armstrong becomes first man to walk on the moon.

1969 Massive rock concert in Woodstock, N.Y. attracts half a million young people.

1970 Four students are killed by National Guardsmen during war protest at Kent State University.

1971 Busing as means of achieving desegregation of schools is upheld by U.S. Supreme Court.

1971 Texas Instruments makes first pocket calculator.

1972 President Nixon is first U.S. President ever to visit China.

1972 Nixon–Brezhnev summit in Russia results in signing of Strategic Arms Limitation Treaty (SALT), initiating era of detente.

1973 In *Roe* v. *Wade*, U.S. Supreme Court defends women's right to privacy as basis for invalidating state laws restricting abortion in first trimester.

1973 Accord signed by U.S. and North Vietnam officially ends American combat role in war. South Vietnam surrenders with fall of Saigon in 1975.

1974 Pres. Nixon resigns to avoid certain impeachment for his role in the Watergate scandal.

1975 E.L. Doctorow publishes *Ragtime*.

1976 U.S. spacecraft *Viking 1* and *2* land on Mars.

1978 Isaac Bashevis Singer wins Nobel Prize for such works as *Gimpel the Fool* (1957).

1978 Residents in Love Canal, N.Y. evacuate their homes, fleeing industrial waste.

1979 Accident at Three-Mile Island nuclear power plant forces evacuation of area.

1979 Fifty-two Americans at U.S. embassy in Iran are held hostage.

1980 Supreme Court rules that organisms created through recently-developed genetic engineering may be patented.

1980 Banking industry is deregulated.

1981 Iran releases 52 American hostages only a few minutes after Ronald Reagan is sworn in as 40th President.

1981 Debut flight of reusable shuttle space craft, *Columbia*, takes 54.5 hours.

1981 Acquired Immune Deficiency Syndrome (AIDS) is officially identified in U.S. where by late 1991 more than 125,000 fatalities have occurred.

1981 IBM P.C. is first marketed.

1982 Anne Tyler publishes *Dinner at the Homesick Restaurant. The Accidental Tourist* follows in 1985.

1982 Barney Clark receives first artificial heart transplant, the Jarvik-7.

1985 U.S. becomes net debtor nation for the first time since 1914.

1986 U.S. Supreme Court upholds affirmative action as remedy of past discrimination against women and minorities.

1986 Sales of arms to Iran and diversion of profits to Nicaraguan Contras are revealed.

1987 Reagan and Gorbachev sign Intermediate Nuclear Forces (INF) Treaty providing for dismantling of all intermediate range nuclear weapons.

1989 U.S. government decides to bail out nation's ailing savings-and-loan banks.

1991 In war in the Persian Gulf, U.S.-led U.N. forces drive Iraq from Kuwait.

1991 Banking industry and Wall Street are shaken by scandals.

1991 U.S. recognizes Baltics as Soviet Union disintegrates.

1991 After bitter controversy and accusations of sexual harassment, Clarence Thomas is confirmed as 106th justice of the U.S. Supreme Court.

The Spanish Century

I T IS ONE OF THE COMMONPLACES of history that the European discovery of the Western Hemisphere came about accidentally, an unexpected result of the search for an ocean route to the Orient. Europeans had traded in a limited way with China centuries before Columbus—since the days of Marco Polo in the thirteenth century, some intrepid European travelers and merchants had found their way to the Orient—but the trip was long and arduous, whether overland or partly along the seacoasts of Asia, and the volume of trade that could ever be achieved that way was obviously negligible. Even the limited access to China afforded Westerners by the routes these travelers used was lost after the rise of the hostile Ottoman Turkish Empire in the fourteenth century; trade with China ceased for almost two hundred years before the Portuguese reopened it by sailing around the coast of Africa at the same time that Columbus was sailing to the West Indies for Spain. An early printed copy of Marco Polo's *Travels*, which Columbus owned, survives, a reminder of how strongly he felt the lure of the riches of the Orient. He came to believe that he could obtain them by sailing west across the Atlantic.

While Columbus shared the belief, relatively widespread in the educated circles of his day, that the earth was round, he had one major geographical misconception which gave him confidence that he could reach the Orient by sailing westward. Underestimating the size of the earth, he believed that China was much closer to Europe than it is. When he set out in 1492, Columbus thought he would have to sail less than 4,000 miles to reach the Orient, not much more than he actually sailed to reach the West Indies. When he discovered the West Indies, he thought he had indeed landed at some isolated outcropping of the fabled East; he died in Spain in 1506, after four voyages to the West Indies, still firm in this belief. The idea soon took hold in Europe, however, that what he had found was a previously unknown land between Europe and Asia. Less than a decade after Columbus's death, Balboa crossed Central America at present-day Panama and discovered the Pacific Ocean; the successful circumnavigation of the earth by Magellan's expedition, completed in 1522, confirmed this new knowledge.

That it was Spain which discovered the Western Hemisphere and took the leading role in the early decades of its exploration owed something to chance. Portugal, under the leadership of Henry the Navigator earlier in the fifteenth century, had become the most enterprising seagoing European nation, but their efforts were concentrated southward, exploring the west coast of Africa. By 1487, the Portuguese had reached the southern tip of Africa, establishing the groundwork for Vasco da Gama's successful 1497 expedition around the Cape of Good Hope to India. During that period, Columbus approached the Portuguese King with his plan to reach the Orient by sailing west; his plan was rejected. Columbus then turned to Spain for sponsorship. After presenting his proposal to Ferdinand and Isabella in 1486, Columbus had to wait for years while a special commission studied his plans, and while he negotiated his share of the potential rewards of the expedition. Agreement was reached, clearing the way for his first voyage, only in the early months of 1492.

Portugal's overseas interests eventually did reach the New World almost in spite of themselves when Pedro Alvares Cabral, off course on a voyage to India, landed on the coast of Brazil on April 22, 1500. Potential conflict between Spain and Portugal in the New World had been provided for and was avoided by the 1494 Treaty of Tordesillas which gave Spain everything west of a north/south line 1,275 miles west of the Azores, and Portugal control east of that line. By this treaty Portugal's control of the sea routes to the Orient around Africa—their prime concern—was maintained, and six years before Cabral accidentally landed there, the Atlantic "bulge" of Brazil was providentially established as the only potential area of Portuguese influence in the Western Hemisphere.

During his four voyages to the West Indies between 1492 and 1504, Columbus explored many Caribbean islands and, on his third voyage in 1498–1500, touched the mainland of South America. He gave Spain a foothold in the Western Hemisphere which others soon came to exploit. Puerto Rico, Jamaica, and Cuba were explored and conquered between 1509 and 1511, in the same period that Vasco Nuñez de Balboa established, at Darien on the Isthmus of Panama, the first successful colony on the South American continent. Hernando Cortés became for all time the symbol of the Spanish conquistador when he brilliantly conquered the Aztec Empire and gave Mexico to Spain in 1519–21. Two decades later Francisco Vazquez de Coronado left New Spain, as conquered Mexico was then called, on his historic mission through America's Southwest as far north as present-day Kansas. Francisco Pizarro, who had been with Balboa at the discovery of the Pacific in 1513, captured the Spanish imagination when he conquered the Inca Empire of Peru in 1531–33. On the North American mainland, Ponce de León, intrigued by the legend of the Fountain of Youth, claimed Florida for Spain in 1513; he returned on a second expedition in 1521, only to be killed by the Seminoles. Twenty years later, Hernando de Soto used Florida as the starting point for the expedition which discovered the Mississippi River; like so many of his countrymen, de Soto came to explore America and was buried here.

A brief listing of voyages and conquests does little to make clear the jarring clash of cultures which the events of these decades represented; the Spanish position in the New World was only achieved at the cost of devastating violence perpetrated on the native populations of the Western Hemisphere. Those who survived encounters with heavily armed and ruthless Spanish soldiers still had to contend with diseases imported from Europe against which they were unprotected. The syphilis which the Spanish brought back from America and introduced into Europe in the early years of the sixteenth century was certainly disastrous to a European population among whom it had been previously unknown, but the numbers affected hardly compare to the millions of native Americans wiped out by the smallpox, measles, dysentery, typhoid, tuberculosis and other European diseases which the conquering nations brought west with them.

Preoccupied with European politics, France played a limited role in the exploration of the Western Hemisphere in the decades following Columbus's discovery. Jacques Cartier's voyages to the Gulf of St. Lawrence in 1534, 1535, and 1541, failed to find a northern passage to Asia, but did establish France's later claims to Canada. English efforts in the decades following 1492 were sporadic and often met with misfortune. John Cabot—born Giovanni Caboto, a native of Genoa like Columbus—sailing under the English flag, reached the New World in 1497 and landed either in southern Labrador, Newfoundland, or Cape Breton Island. A second expedition, however, left little record and may have been lost at sea, as Cabot himself simply disappears from history. Martin Frobisher led three voyages to the northeast coast of Canada in 1576–78, but found neither gold nor a route to the Pacific, and failed to establish a successful colony. Sir Francis Drake completed England's first circumnavigation in 1577–80, but his landing near present-day San Francisco had little impact on the history of America. Sir Humphrey Gilbert led a major colonizing expedition to Newfoundland in 1583, but his five ships and 260 men went down in a storm in the North Atlantic. Following Gilbert's debacle, the English looked south for more favorable weather, but their immediate luck proved no better there. Sir Walter Raleigh established an English colony at Roanoke Island off the coast of North Carolina, where on August 18, 1587, Virginia Dare, the first child of English parents in the Western Hemisphere, was born; by 1590, however, the Roanoke settlers had vanished without a trace.

■ A nineteenth-century painting by Edward A. Abbey of **Christopher Columbus** *(above)* landing in the New World. Financed by the King and Queen of Spain, Columbus sailed on his first voyage, with the *Niña, Pinta* and *Santa María,* from Palos on August 3, 1492, searching for a western route to the Far East. Land was sighted—it turned out to be San Salvador—on October 12. On his second voyage, 1493–1496, Columbus founded the first permanent city to be established by Europeans in the New World, Isabella on Hispaniola, but the expedition met many misfortunes. On his third voyage, he reached the mainland of South America (in present-day Venezuela), but returned to Spain as a prisoner because of the failure of his administration of the new Spanish colonies. After a final voyage to the West Indies in 1502–04, during which he was marooned on Jamaica for over a year, Columbus died in Spain on May 20, 1506, still believing he had found the East Indies.

■ A contemporary engraving of the Florentine navigator **Amerigo Vespucci** *(right)* using an astrolabe to locate the Southern Cross. Vespucci was an officer on three voyages to the Western Hemisphere between 1499 and 1507 which primarily explored the coast of Brazil. He published a book shortly after the last voyage which made wildly extravagant claims for his discoveries, among them that he found the American mainland before Columbus. The cartographer Martin Waldseemüller erroneously accepted Vespucci's narrative, and when in 1507 he published the first map showing the Western Hemisphere as a distinct land mass between Europe and Asia, Waldseemüller named the new land America. The name was adopted by other writers and cartographers despite Vespucci's limited role in the discovery and exploration of the New World.

■ The Spanish explorer **Francisco Vásquez de Coronado** *(left)* departed present-day Mexico in February, 1540 with a troop of 400 Spaniards and about 1,000 natives in the hope of finding the legendary Seven Cities of Cibola or the fabulously wealthy land of Quivira. Instead of the mythical Cibola, Coronado found the pueblos of the Zuni Indians in present-day New Mexico. He then penetrated as far north as what is now Kansas before deciding that Quivira was a fable and returning to Mexico in 1542. One of his officers, Captain García López de Cárdenas, leading a secondary expedition, was the first European to discover the Grand Canyon.

■ **Juan Ponce de León** *(right, top)* in a fanciful illustration of his search for the fabled Fountain of Youth. History doesn't record that de León, who had sailed on Columbus's second voyage, ever found the Fountain, but he did claim Florida in the name of the King of Spain in 1513.

■ A nineteenth-century engraving of the Spanish explorer **Hernando de Soto** *(right, bottom)* discovering the Mississippi River on May 8, 1541. De Soto landed with 600 soldiers from Spanish Cuba on the west coast of Florida in May, 1539, with plans to search new territories for gold. Though like many explorers in the New World he never found gold, de Soto did explore vast tracts of previously unknown wilderness before coming across the river that would be named the Mississippi. De Soto and his troops explored west of the Mississippi for a year before he died of a fever on May 21, 1542. He was buried in the mud at the bottom of the Mississippi.

■ **Giovanni da Verrazano** *(left),* Florentine navigator who sailed under the French flag and explored the coast of North America in 1524 in his ship *La Dauphine.* Verrazano examined hundreds of miles of the Atlantic coastline of North America, from Cape Fear, North Carolina to as far north as Cape Breton, Nova Scotia. On April 17, 1524 he sighted what was to become New York harbor, later describing both the natives and the magnificent river which would be named after Henry Hudson. Verrazano himself was commemorated in 1964 when the world's longest suspension bridge (at that time), the Verrazano-Narrows Bridge, was opened between Brooklyn and Staten Island, New York.

■ In 1580 **Sir Francis Drake** *(right)* completed the voyage which made him the first Englishman to circumnavigate the globe. This nineteenth-century engraving shows Drake greeting friendly Indians in California after he came ashore in June, 1579 at what would be named San Francisco Bay. Drake remained there a month—during which he conducted the first Protestant religious services in the New World—refitting his ship, *The Golden Hind,* and preparing for the return voyage to England. Queen Elizabeth I knighted Drake on his return, and in 1588 he played a major role in the defeat of the Spanish Armada.

*"O my America!
my new-found land."*

—JOHN DONNE

The English Colonies

THE HISTORY OF AMERICA has always been tied to European politics. Consolidation of royal power in Spain enabled the Spanish, at the end of the fifteenth century, to dedicate their energies and resources to exploration and conquest in the New World. In the following century, while the Spanish themselves remained uninterested in the area north of Mexico, their powerful navy inhibited others from colonizing North America. With the defeat and destruction of the Spanish Armada by the English in 1588, the way was finally open for the English especially to spread their nautical wings westward. The English outlook toward the New World was fundamentally different from the Spanish. The Spanish sent armed expeditions to America to claim new lands, to establish settlements, but primarily to bring back riches. The English instead claimed the land which their early travelers visited, and granted huge tracts of it to individuals or companies who undertook to find settlers and establish colonies there. Many were eager to go to America; some sought economic opportunity or cheap land to farm, some sought religious freedom, some sought adventure, some were one step ahead of the sheriff or a sentence to debtor's prison. For all of these reasons, thousands came to North America during the seventeenth century.

The first successful English colony in America was established at Jamestown, Virginia in 1607, and did not have an easy time sustaining itself—Indian attacks, disease, and hunger marked Virginia's first years, and to attract new settlers the Virginia Company was by 1618 offering 50 free acres of land to those who could pay for their transportation from England, and to those who couldn't, the promise of 50 free acres after seven years. Two features of life in early Virginia which foreshadowed later events were the establishment of a tobacco industry as early as 1612 and the organization of the House of Burgesses, the first legislative body in America, which convened for the first time in Jamestown in July, 1619.

Just north of Virginia, the first colonists in Maryland had a very different experience. The land which became Maryland had been granted not to a joint-stock company, but to a single individual, Lord Baltimore, whose younger brother, Leonard Calvert, landed with the first settlers on St. Clement's (now Blakistone) Island in the lower Potomac in March, 1634. They quickly established peace with the local Indians, and harvested a successful crop of corn their first year; Maryland prospered from the start. Under the leadership of the Catholic Calvert family, Maryland became a center of religious freedom compared with colonies where the governing bodies were closely tied to one or another Puritan sect and all too ready to anathematize any dissidents. Freedom of religion, albeit only within the bounds of trinitarian Christianity, was formalized in Maryland in 1649 when the General Assembly passed the famous Act of Religious Toleration. In later years, however, a Puritan controlled assembly pushed through laws penalizing the practice of Catholicism.

The settlement of New England in the seventeenth century represents a facet of the spread of the Protestant Reformation. In England, the Reformation gave rise to many different sects of Puritans—those who wished to purify established religion of what each sect considered erroneous practices—which inevitably found themselves in conflict with the Anglican church. Against the elaborate ceremonies and complicated church hierarchy of the established Anglicans, the Puritan sects stressed the study of the Bible and, though with many differences in emphasis among them, required steady churchgoing, good works, diligence in one's daily calling, and a properly reverent attitude toward ministers. Some English Puritans left for countries such as the Netherlands, where they hoped to find toleration, and some eventually came to see America as a place where they might be able to build new societies governed according to their beliefs. Their austere struggles to build, in their own words "a Zion in the wilderness" gave early New England life its special character.

The early history of Massachusetts centers around two distinct colonies, the one established at Plymouth by the Pilgrims who arrived on the Mayflower in 1620, and the Massachusetts Bay colony proper, founded in 1630. The Pilgrims were Puritan religious refugees from England who had been living in Leyden, Holland; as "separatists," they didn't seek to reform the Church of England, but wanted to break away from it to form their own community. Though never a majority of the Plymouth colony, the Pilgrims, under their forceful leader William Bradford, totally controlled its government. The Mayflower Compact, which all 41 adult males on the ship had signed, promised that the signers would abide by the laws drafted by the leaders of the colony. It was hardly a democratic document, calling for rule by the elite, but it did establish the idea that political authority properly derives from the consent of the governed, and thus it was a stage, if a primitive one, in the evolution of America's political institutions.

The Puritans of Massachusetts Bay were not separatists; they desired to reform the established church from within. This did not make them tolerant of diverging beliefs. On the contrary, a prominent feature of life in Massachusetts Bay was the authoritarian nature of Puritanism practiced there. Dissidents from Massachusetts Bay, such as the group the Rev. Thomas Hooker took to the Connecticut Valley in 1635, were continually being expelled into the New England wilderness where they founded new colonies. Around the same time, Rhode Island was established by Roger Williams and others who were also expelled from Massachusetts Bay.

The Dutch West India Company founded New Netherland on Manhattan Island in 1624; the English captured it in 1664, lost it back to the Dutch in 1673, and recaptured it for good the following year. Pennsylvania, the Quaker colony founded by William Penn, who received his grant of land along the Delaware River from Charles II in 1681 in payment of a debt of sixteen thousand pounds owed by the King to Penn's father, was a prosperous colony from the start, marked by religious toleration, at least for all Protestants, and a powerful, elected legislative body. Colonizing began in the Carolinas in the 1660s, but got off to a shaky start. The leaders of the first settlements hoped to grow silk in the warm Carolina climate; this idea failed completely. A series of costly Indian wars made it difficult to attract settlers until well into the eighteenth century, at which time Georgia was founded explicitly as a place where imprisoned English debtors could rehabilitate themselves. New Jersey was established as a separate English colony in 1665.

England was not operating alone on the North American continent in the seventeenth century. Samuel de Champlain established a French colony at Quebec in 1608; two years later the Spanish set up Santa Fe as the capital of the province of New Mexico. Champlain reached Lake Ontario in 1615 and Lake Superior in 1622; Jean Nicolet, another Frenchman, found Lake Michigan in 1634, but still nurturing Columbus's dream, returned to Quebec disappointed that he hadn't reached the Orient. Nicolet at least returned; Etienne Brulé, a companion of Champlain on the expeditions to Lakes Ontario and Superior, was killed and eaten by the Huron Indians in 1633. The French and English would settle their differences over supremacy in North America on the battlefield in the following century.

The major drama of the seventeenth century in North America was the establishment of English colonies up and down the length of the Atlantic seacoast from present-day Maine to South Carolina. They formed a patchwork of political, economic and religious institutions. Some practiced religious toleration; others were rigid and suspicious of any divergence in practice or belief. Some were characterized by small farms worked mostly by their owners; others had already witnessed the beginnings of a slave-owning plantation economy. Some had powerful urban centers with an active class of commercial entrepreneurs; others were almost totally rural. Inland areas were still unknown; as the seventeenth century closed, the Allegheny Mountains and the Ohio River were still far beyond the western horizon.

■ Lithograph *(opposite, top)* of the marriage in April, 1614 between the Powhatan Indian princess **Pocahontas** and Englishman John Rolfe. Few events in the early history of America are as steeped in romance as the story of Pocahontas. English settlers led by Captain John Smith landed at Chesapeake Bay on April 26, 1607 and soon established their colony at Jamestown. A few years later, in the story which derives from Smith's own later account, Smith and his exploring party were captured by the Powhatan Indians, who planned to execute him. Smith's life was saved by Pocahontas, the 13-year old daughter of the chief. After Smith's return to England in 1609, relations between the Indians and the Jamestown settlers worsened. Pocahontas was captured by a settler, Captain Samuel Argall, who hoped to use her to negotiate a favorable peace. Before she could be ransomed and returned to her tribe, she met and fell in love with Rolfe. Their marriage, which had her father's approval, established peace as long as Pocahontas lived. On a trip to England with her husband in 1616, part of a scheme to interest prospective settlers in Virginia, Pocahontas was warmly received by the English court and society. She contracted smallpox, however, and died and was buried in England in 1617. Her son Thomas Rolfe later emigrated to Virginia.

■ The title page *(opposite, bottom left)* of **an advertisement for colonists to Virginia,** printed in London in 1609.

■ A nineteenth-century engraving *(opposite, bottom right)* of the **Pilgrim Fathers** praying before leaving Southampton, England in 1620 in search of freedom from religious persecution. The Pilgrims, members of the English Separatist Church, a branch of Puritanism, landed in the *Mayflower* on November 21, 1620 near present-day Provincetown on Cape Cod. On December 26 they reached Plymouth where they established the first permanent colony in New England—their plan had been to settle in Virginia, but storms on the rough Atlantic crossing forced them north. The 102 colonists, only 35 of whom were members of the Separatist Church, did not describe themselves as Pilgrims; the term "Pilgrim Fathers" only became common 200 years later after orator Daniel Webster used it in a speech at a commemorative celebration.

"Come ye thankful people, come,
Raise the song of Harvest-home;
All is safely gathered in,
Ere the winter storms begin."

—HENRY ALFORD

■ **The first Thanksgiving** *(below)*, from a nineteenth-century painting. William Bradford, Governor of the Plymouth Colony, ordered a thanksgiving feast to be held in the fall of 1621 to mark the survival of the colony through its first, difficult winter, and the abundant corn crop harvested that fall which augured well for the future. The colonists were joined by Chief Massasoit and 99 of his braves from the Wampanoag tribe in what proved also to be a celebration of their friendly relations. Thanksgiving immediately became a New England tradition.

■ **Henry Hudson's ship *Half Moon*** (*top*), sailing up the Hudson River. Searching for a passage to the Pacific, Hudson went north in 1609 and 1610 up the river which is named for him. In the winter of 1610, Hudson's crew mutinied in what is now Hudson Bay and set him adrift with a few loyal sailors. Hudson was never heard from again.

■ **Peter Minuit** (*middle*) buying Manhattan Island on behalf of the Dutch from the Canarsee Indians in 1626 for 60 guilders (the legendary $24.00) in beads and other trinkets. A year earlier the Dutch had established their colony, New Amsterdam, at the foot of Manhattan Island.

■ **William Penn** (*bottom*) agreeing to a treaty with the Indians after the establishment of the Quaker colony of Pennsylvania in 1682. This Currier and Ives lithograph, showing Penn and the Indians signing their 1683 peace treaty at Shackamaxon, follows in overall design a well-known early American painting by Benjamin West, *Penn's Peace Treaty With the Indians*, painted in 1771.

■ A later drawing of the French Jesuit Father **Jacques Marquette** (*opposite, top left*) who in 1674 explored 2,500 miles of the Mississippi River with fur trader Louis Joliet. In 1668 Marquette had established at Sault Sainte Marie the first permanent colony in Michigan.

■ French explorer **René Robert Cavelier, sieur de La Salle** (*opposite, bottom left*), claiming the Mississippi Valley for France on April 9, 1682 on arriving at the mouth of the Mississippi after a four-month journey from Fort Miami on Lake Michigan. La Salle, who named the new territory Louisiana after Louis XIV, was killed by his own men in a mutiny while exploring the coastline of the Gulf of Mexico on March 19, 1687.

■ A Howard Pyle illustration of the 1692 **Salem Witch Trials** *(below)*. Nineteen convicted witches were hanged, and one man pressed to death with a stone. The trials were the culmination of a series of events which began with the frenzied reaction of some local young girls to tales of voodoo magic related to them by a family slave from the West Indies. Stimulated by the fabulous stories they heard, so incredible in the cold and dour atmosphere of Puritan New England, the girls claimed they were possessed by the Devil and began accusing their neighbors of practicing witchcraft. Local authorities, urged by the Puritan clergy, set up a special court to investigate the charges. Accusations, denials, and counteraccusations resulted in an astonishing series of executions of those who refused to confess to being witches. Before long, reason prevailed, the trials were stopped, and their injustice was publicly admitted.

■ **Harvard College** *(top)* in Colonial times. Harvard, the first college in America, was founded 1636, only sixteen years after the Pilgrims reached Plymouth. The new college, sponsored in its early years by the Puritan Church, was named for a Puritan minister, John Harvard, who left the college his library of 400 volumes and half his estate, 780 pounds sterling. Harvard opened its doors in 1638 with one master teaching classes in a small frame house in New Towne, later renamed Cambridge after the English university John Harvard had attended.

"Yet America is a poem in our eyes; its ample geography dazzles the imagination, and it will not wait long for metres."

—RALPH WALDO EMERSON

■ Franciscan missionary **Louis Hennepin** *(bottom),* who accompanied La Salle to Canada in 1675. In 1678 they became the first Europeans to see Niagara Falls. They established Ft. Crèvecoeur on the site of present-day Peoria, Illinois in 1680, and Hennepin later reached the site of Minneapolis. After returning to France in 1682, Hennepin wrote the first published description of this territory, *Description de la Louisiane* (1683), but his false claim in a later account to have explored the Mississippi to its mouth has cast suspicion on his other disclosures.

Toward Independence

AMERICA'S EVENTUAL INDEPENDENCE from Great Britain was inevitable. In the first decades of the seventeenth century, a few ships carrying a hundred or two hundred people at a time crossed the Atlantic bringing the first settlers to the New World. There were frequent setbacks, but despite the difficulties, the colonies grew. By 1650, the population of the British colonies in America had reached 52,000. By the end of the century, this figure had multiplied five times, to 250,000. By 1760, the population of the Colonies had almost reached 1,700,000. It is difficult to imagine, whatever course they followed, that Britain could have remained in control forever of this constantly expanding population in a distant hemisphere, in a country many times larger than Britain itself, with a seemingly limitless frontier to the west waiting to be explored.

The conflicts over trade, shipping, and taxation which erupted at Lexington and Concord in April, 1775 had their origins in a much earlier time. In 1660, England had passed a Navigation Act requiring that goods being shipped to England or to the English colonies, whatever their origin, be shipped in English ships, and that certain commodities produced in the Colonies, such as sugar, cotton, and tobacco, be shipped only to England; trade in these "enumerated articles" with other nations was prohibited. Colonial trade with England was not a minor matter; by the decade of the 1760s, American goods exported to England were valued at more than a million English pounds sterling annually, with almost twice that much being imported from England to America; this was four times the volume of trade in the first decade of the eighteenth century. Foreign trade was crucial to the economic life of the Colonies; conflict over the right to regulate it, tax it, and profit from it, led directly to the Revolution.

Other factors leading to the political break with England included the development of independent political institutions in the Colonies. Colonial legislative assemblies, of which the most famous was Virginia's House of Burgesses, developed gradually into powerful institutions which effectively limited the power of the royal governors. Usually dominated by the richest and most powerful local families, these provincial legislative bodies provided a forum for the expression of discontent with the government in London. In 1775 the idea of overthrowing a royal government by force was not as outlandish as it might seem; the English themselves had overthrown the Stuart Monarchy in the previous century, and had formulated an appealing political philosophy deriving from the ideas of John Locke and others that power must be based on the consent of the governed, and could be forfeited if exercised in an arbitrary or capricious way. It was only a short leap to the idea that the most desirable political order would be established in an independent nation, particularly when the framers of the Declaration of Independence had been able to append to their opening statement a lengthy list of grievances against the King of England.

It is one of history's paradoxes that the loss of her American colonies happened just after, and partly as a result of, England's victory in the French and Indian War, which between 1756 and 1763 established England's control over North America. The 1763 Treaty of Paris gave England all of Canada and other territory once claimed by France east of the Mississippi River; never had England's position in the Western Hemisphere seemed so secure. However, the cost of the war had been high, effectively more than doubling the total annual expenditures of the English government. To help pay for that war the English government would turn to the Colonies and attempt to impose new revenue-producing taxes there; now that the war had eliminated the threat posed by the French and their Indian allies, however, the Colonies felt less inclined than ever to bear the burden of England's military establishment.

Reaction to the Stamp Act of 1765 varied from a boycott in some areas against all English imports to the assembling of a congress of delegates from nine colonies in New York in October, 1765 which sent protests about the new taxes to England. The boycott and the protests worked, and the Stamp Act was repealed at the same time that the English Parliament issued the face-saving Declaratory Act asserting their right to legislate for the Colonies in all areas. Shortly thereafter, in June 1767, the English tried again with the Townshend Duties, which imposed taxes on paper, paint, lead, glass and, most important, tea imported to the Colonies. Another boycott ensued, and all of the Townshend Duties except the one on tea were repealed. The 1773 Tea Act, designed to shore up the financially troubled East India Company by allowing English tea to be sold more cheaply in America than the popular varieties imported by the Dutch, rekindled earlier antagonisms and led directly to the Boston Tea Party of December, 1773, when a cargo of British tea was destroyed in Boston Harbor. Parliament responded with the series of punitive measures known in the Colonies as the Intolerable Acts.

The First Continental Congress in 1774 sent a list of colonial grievances to the King of England and called for continued boycotts of English trade. In New England, the colonials drilled themselves into units of minutemen—ready on a moment's notice—and found themselves in action at Lexington and Concord in April, 1775 after Paul Revere's famous ride warning of British troop movements against the colonials' stores of arms. That summer Washington was named Commander-in-Chief of the Continental Army by the Second Continental Congress assembled at Philadelphia, and the first steps toward securing the alliance of France were taken. In the summer of 1776, in the midst of the war, Congress passed the Declaration of Independence, which set forth in detail the principles on which the new nation would be based.

The early years of the war provided mixed results. The British scored a victory at Bunker Hill in 1775, but the following spring were forced to evacuate Boston. In June 1776, the British failed in their attempt to take Charleston, the leading southern port, but later that summer, routed the Americans in the Battle of Long Island, after which the American army barely escaped across the East River to Manhattan. Washington struck back at Trenton and Princeton after his famous crossing of the Delaware on Christmas night, 1776. Horatio Gates's victory over British General Burgoyne at Saratoga in October, 1777 provided the turning point, particularly because it convinced the French that the English could be beaten, and brought them into the war on the side of the Americans. After four more long years of fighting, the main British army under Cornwallis surrendered at Yorktown, Virginia on October 29, 1781.

The Articles of Confederation which joined the states together after the Revolution failed to provide the new Republic with the necessary cohesiveness, especially in the economic sphere, which many thought could be attained with a stronger central government. Delegates from twelve of the thirteen original states—Rhode Island failed to send a delegate—convened in Philadelphia in the summer of 1787 and drafted the Constitution of the United States. A wide-ranging campaign over political ideals followed as citizens in every state debated the new plan. The famous series of *Federalist Papers* by James Madison, Alexander Hamilton, and John Jay rallied support for the Constitution, which would be effective when ratified by nine states. Delaware was the first, on December 7, 1787; New Hampshire became the crucial ninth on June 21, 1788. By May 29, 1790, when Rhode Island joined the fold, all of the original thirteen states had ratified. The Constitution went into effect on the first Wednesday in March, 1789 with George Washington as President. Fear that too much power had been granted to the government led to the preparation of the first ten amendments to the Constitution, the Bill of Rights, ratified on December 15, 1791. With its new government in place, its advantageous situation secure from the effects of the volatile European politics of the era of the French Revolution, the new nation headed more or less blindly into a century of unexpected and unimaginable conflict, expansion, growth, and change beyond anyone's wildest dreams.

■ An engraving of **James Oglethorpe** *(top)* meeting with local Indians. In 1733 Oglethorpe arrived from England with 35 families, including many with members just released from debtor's prison, to found the new colony of Georgia, named after George II.

■ **Cotton Mather** *(below),* an engraving after a painting by Peter Pelham. Son of Puritan minister Increase Mather, Cotton Mather entered Harvard at the age of twelve, in 1675, and began preaching at seventeen. He published a vast number of theological works, many dealing with witchcraft, a consuming public issue of his time. Mather defended the verdicts reached at the Salem witch trials. In a more enlightened vein, he campaigned for innoculation against smallpox, an unpopular cause in his day. The several generations of Mather ministers wielded tremendous influence during the years when Puritanism ruled Boston and New England.

■ A leading explorer and administrator of French North America, **Antoine Laumet de La Mothe, sieur de Cadillac,** *(bottom),* leading an exploring party. Cadillac founded the city of Detroit as a military outpost in 1701 and named it *Fort-Pontchartrain du Détroit* (of the strait), after Louis XIV's minister of state, comte de Pontchartrain. Cadillac later served as governor of French Louisiana.

"America is a tune. It must be sung together."

—GERARD STANLEY LEE

■ A scene from the **French and Indian War** *(opposite, top),* drawn by military specialist Rufus Zogbaum for *Harper's Weekly* at the end of the 19th century. The war from 1756 to 1763 was part of the world-wide struggle between England and France which dominated international politics in the 18th century. In the early years of the conflict over whether England or France would predominate in North America, the French with their Indian allies often proved a formidable opponent. By the end of 1757, the English had begun to turn the tide with a series of important victories which culminated in the fall of Quebec in September, 1759. A year later all of Canada was under British control. Ironically, the French and Indian War provided a chance for many colonial officers on the English side, including then Col. George Washington, to gain experience which would later be used against the British in the American Revolution.

■ George Caleb Bingham's 1851 painting of **Daniel Boone** *(opposite, bottom)* leading his own family and other settlers through the Cumberland Gap in the Appalachian Mountains near the juncture of Virginia, Tennessee and Kentucky. Boone brought several families through the Cumberland Gap to Kentucky in 1773, but the group was turned back by Indians. Boone's son James was killed on this expedition. Two years later Boone and his companions blazed the Wilderness Road from eastern Virginia to the interior of Kentucky, opening the area to settlement despite continued Indian attacks. Shortly thereafter, Boone brought his family to what came to be called Boonesborough, the first permanent settlement in Kentucky. A hunter and trapper, Boone died in 1820 in Missouri where he lived after 1799; his legendary fame partly rests on the stanzas of Byron's *Don Juan* (1823) devoted to his exploits.

To the Public.

THE long expected TEA SHIP arrived last night at Sandy-Hook, but the pilot would not bring up the Captain till the sense of the city was known. The committee were immediately informed of her arrival, and that the Captain solicits for liberty to come up to provide necessaries for his return. The ship to remain at Sandy-Hook. The committee conceiving it to be the sense of the city that he should have such liberty, signified it to the Gentleman who is to supply him with provisions, and other necessaries. Advice of this was immediately dispatched to the Captain; and whenever he comes up, care will be taken that he does not enter at the custom-house, and that no time be lost in dispatching him.

New-York, April 19, 1774.

■ **The Boston Tea Party** *(top).* On December 16, 1773, in protest against the English government's Tea Act, which earlier in the year had placed an unwelcome tax on the colonials' favorite beverage, a group of Bostonians, thinly disguised as Indians, boarded three British East India Company tea ships and threw 342 cases of taxable tea into Boston Harbor. Tension between colonials and Parliament continued to escalate when in response the English government passed a new series of punitive measures known in the colonies as the Intolerable Acts.

■ Agitation over tea was not confined to Boston as seen in this **1774 broadside** *(above left)* concerning events in New York City.

■ **The Boston Massacre** *(above right)* was an earlier incident in the struggle between the citizens of Boston and the British government over the right to tax. A crowd protesting new taxes called for by the Townshend Acts confronted a detachment of British troops on March 5, 1770. In response to rocks and ice thrown by the crowd, the soldiers opened fire. Five protestors, including Crispus Attucks, a black sailor and former slave, were killed. The officer in charge, defended in court by John Adams, was acquitted of murder, but the unpopular Townshend Acts were largely repealed. This print by Paul Revere, an effective piece of anti-British propaganda, circulated widely in the years leading up to the Revolution.

"This destruction of the tea is so bold, so daring, so firm, intrepid and inflexible, and it must have so important consequences, and so lasting, that I can't but consider it as an epocha in history!"

—JOHN ADAMS

■ **A Massachusetts treasury note** of 1775 *(top left)*. As the authority of the British began to be challenged, notes such as this— "issued in defense of American liberty"— began to circulate in the colonies.

■ An undated engraving of the famous ride of **Paul Revere** *(top right)*. On the night of April 18, 1775 Revere rode to warn the minutemen that the British troops were marching from Boston; the next morning, the inexperienced but determined colonials were ready for action at Lexington and Concord. Revere was a master silversmith and engraver who took a leading role in the political struggles of pre-Revolutionary War Boston. One of the participants in the Boston Tea Party, Revere served the Boston Committee of Safety—the anti-British political organization—as a rider, journeying sometimes as far as New York and Philadelphia to exchange information with similar groups.

■ **A British sympathizer** *(bottom left)* being drummed out of an American village, a typical incident of the Revolutionary period, in a wood engraving by C.S. Reinhart, a late-19th century *Harper's Weekly* artist.

■ **A British cartoon of 1774** *(bottom right)* showing how the authority of the English government was disregarded in the colonies. Tea is being forced down the throat of the tarred and feathered English tax collector while the Stamp Act is nailed upside down on the Liberty Tree.

■ Minutemen at Concord Bridge *(right),* as the American Revolution began on April 19, 1775. After a brief skirmish at Lexington, 11 miles northwest of Boston, the first major battle of the Revolution took place at Concord's North Bridge, eight miles from Lexington, as a troop of several hundred British regulars attempting to reach an arms depot at Concord were harassed from all sides and forced to retreat by the hastily assembled colonial minutemen. Seventy-three British soldiers and forty-nine colonials were killed.

■ An engraving after John Trumbull's painting of **The Battle of Bunker Hill** *(below).* American forces outside Boston where the British were entrenched meant to fortify Bunker Hill on June 16, 1775, but by mistake they fortified Breed's Hill, lower, closer to Boston and more vulnerable to shelling. The British attacked the next day and drove the Americans from their position after three assaults and hand-to-hand combat. Over a thousand British soldiers were killed. The Americans' strong resistance to the well-trained British regulars—a few hundred colonials were killed—made this defeat into a moral victory and one of the legends of the early days of the nation.

■ **The Spirit of '76** *(left),* a painting by Archibald M. Willard. The first battles of the war in New England were fought by the minutemen—so named because they were ready to fight at a moment's notice. The Massachusetts provincial congress had created regiments of minutemen in 1774, and they were ready when the time came at Lexington and Concord. The colonials' military structure became somewhat more organized soon afterward. The Second Continental Congress created the Continental Army in May, 1775. John Adams of Massachusetts presented the unanimous resolution that named George Washington commander on June 15. Within two weeks Washington was in Boston to take charge.

■ **Patrick Henry** *(right)* making his famous "Give me liberty or give me death" speech to Virginia's second revolutionary convention on March 23, 1775, just a few weeks before war began far to the north at Lexington and Concord. A great orator who made his mark ten years earlier in the Virginia House of Burgesses with his "If this be treason, make the most of it" speech, Henry later served as the first governor of Virginia, 1776–1779. He served a second term as governor between 1784 and 1786.

"Is life so dear, or peace so sweet as to be purchased at the price of chains and slavery? Forbid it, Almighty God! I know not what course others may take; but as for me, give me liberty or give me death."

—PATRICK HENRY

"We hold these truths to be self-evident; that all men are created equal . . ."

—THOMAS JEFFERSON

■ The John Trumbull painting *(opposite, top)* which is often called ***The Signing of the Declaration of Independence,*** but which actually portrays the presentation of the Declaration by the committee which prepared it to the Continental Congress at Philadelphia in the summer of 1776. Thomas Jefferson, the principal author of the *Declaration of Independence,* is the figure second from right in the group standing on the left. Trumbull's painting was a group portrait, painted over a period of years well after the event it portrays. Not all of the members of the Continental Congress depicted in it were present either on July 2, when the resolution calling for independence was passed, on July 4, when the formal Declaration was adopted, or on August 2, when most of the members signed it.

■ One of the icons of the Revolutionary War, ***Washington Crossing the Delaware (opposite, bottom),*** painted by Emanuel Leutze in Dusseldorf in 1851. Though the painting is historically inaccurate—the flag depicted was not in use until six months later, the boat is the wrong size and shape, it is doubtful that Washington stood during the rough winter crossing—few images have become so deeply ingrained in the national consciousness. On the night of the actual event, Christmas night of 1776, Washington crossed the Delaware with 2,400 soldiers and 18 pieces of artillery and scored a badly needed victory the next day over the Hessians stationed at Trenton.

■ The execution of **Nathan Hale** *(top)* illustrated by F.O. Darley. No authentic portrait of Hale is known to exist, and his saying before being hanged that he regretted he had only one life to give for his country is almost certainly apocryphal. Hale was captured, disguised as a schoolteacher, while attempting to spy on British forces on Long Island, and executed on September 22, 1776 near present-day First Avenue and 63rd Street in New York City. Under the military protocol of the day, soldiers captured in uniform during the battle were held as prisoners, but spies taken in civilian clothes were subject to execution.

■ Did a Philadelphia seamstress named **Betsy Ross** *(middle)* sew the first stars and stripes? The debate has been going on for over two hundred years with no resolution in sight. Here is a romantic, nineteenth-century conception of Betsy and her flag.

■ George Washington and his great French ally Lafayette at **Valley Forge** *(bottom),* in an engraving after a Chappell painting. Washington's army of 11,000 spent the winter of 1777–1778 in miserable conditions at the Pennsylvania town, 20 miles northwest of Philadelphia. Lafayette came to America to serve in the Continental Army as a volunteer; he played a major role in the later years of the Revolution in successfully encouraging the government of Louis XVI to aid the Americans' cause.

ℳℯ the ℘eople

of the United States, in order to form a more perfect Union, establish Justice, insure domestic Tranquility, provide for the common defence, promote the general Welfare, and secure the Blessings of Liberty to ourselves and our Posterity, do ordain and establish this Constitution for the United States of America.

■ Legend has it that a young American heroine, **Molly Pitcher** *(opposite, top left)*, took over a cannon from her fallen husband at the Battle of Monmouth, New Jersey on June 28, 1778.

■ *The Surrender of Lord Cornwallis at Yorktown*, painted by John Trumbull *(opposite, top right)*. At the mercy of the 16,000-man French and American army, Cornwallis asked Washington for a cease-fire to discuss surrender terms on October 17, 1781, four long years after the military tide began to turn in favor of the Americans at the Battle of Saratoga. On October 19, 1781, the British formally surrendered and laid down their arms. In actuality, Cornwallis did not surrender personally, but sent another general in his place.

■ The Revolutionary War produced its naval heroes as well. This painting, by James Hamilton, depicts the battle between the American ship **Bonhomme Richard** *(opposite, bottom)* named by its Captain, John Paul Jones, in honor of Benjamin Franklin and *Poor Richard's Almanac,* and the British ship *Serapis.* Jones captured the *Serapis* but the *Bonhomme Richard* was so badly damaged it sank two days later. The battle was of little significance, but became one of the Revolution's most frequently illustrated incidents, no doubt because of Jones's colorful personality.

■ **The Preamble to the Constitution** of the United States *(above)*.

■ *Washington Addressing the Constitutional Convention (below),* as painted by J.B. Stearns in 1856. Following the Revolution, the failure of the weak Articles of Confederation led many to desire a stronger central government. Delegates from all the states except Rhode Island met at the Pennsylvania Statehouse in Philadelphia from May 25 to September 17, 1787, as the new Constitution was drafted. Many prominent Americans, including Washington, Franklin, Madison, and others, took part. In one of the most influential political documents ever drafted, the outlines of the new American government were drawn. The major drama was the conflict between those who thought each state should have equal representation in any new Congress and those who thought the larger states should have more votes. In a brilliant compromise suggested by Oliver Ellsworth and Roger Sherman of Connecticut, it was proposed and adopted that the new Congress should have two houses—in one (the Senate) the states would be represented equally, and in the other (the House of Representatives), each state's share of votes would be based on population. The powers of the Federal executive and judiciary branches were also defined. After intense debate throughout the states, the new Constitution was approved by a majority of the original states during the following year.

■ A 1796 portrait of **George Washington** *(left)* by Gilbert Stuart. Washington gained military experience as an officer in the French and Indian War, and later attended both the First and Second Continental Congresses. From June 15, 1775 he was commander of the colonial forces. After such early successes as forcing the British out of Boston in March, 1776, Washington's fortunes on the battlefield had their ups and downs, but he indomitably held the new nation's army together until Yorktown. There was no other choice to be President of the 1787 Constitutional Convention, or first President of the United States. Washington was elected overwhelmingly in 1789 and easily reelected in 1792.

■ **Thomas Jefferson** *(center),* a portrait c. 1791 by Charles Willson Peale. Like Washington, Jefferson was a member of the colonial Virginia political aristocracy. His career began as a member of the House of Burgesses in 1769. He represented Virginia at the Second Continental Congress in 1775 and the following year was chiefly responsible for drafting the Declaration of Independence. After serving as governor of Virginia from 1779 to 1781, Jefferson became the nation's first Secretary of State. Elected as the country's third President in 1801, Jefferson successfully kept the United States, except for a few minor but colorful incidents, from involvement in the Napoleonic Wars. One of his administration's greatest legacies was the conclusion of the Louisiana Purchase from the French in 1803. Jefferson retired from national politics after 1809 and devoted himself to his beloved University of Virginia.

■ **John Adams** *(right)* by Gilbert Stuart. A Boston lawyer who served as a delegate from Massachusetts to the First and Second Continental Congresses, Adams found his role as a diplomat, representing the new nation in the courts of Europe. He was America's first ambassador to Britain, and George Washington's Vice-President. Elected President in 1796, Adams favored a strong central government, but declined to become embroiled, like Washington before him and Jefferson after him, in the volatile political and military strife of Europe during the French Revolution and its aftermath. In one of the ironies of chronology, Adams and Jefferson, collaborators fifty summers before in drafting the Declaration of Independence, died on the same day, July 4, 1826.

"I die hard. But I am not afraid to go."

—GEORGE WASHINGTON

Growth of a Nation

A S THE NINETEENTH CENTURY OPENED, America consisted of the original thirteen states along the eastern coast from New Hampshire to Georgia— Maine was still governed by Massachusetts—plus the four new states of Vermont, Kentucky, Tennessee, and Ohio, which had been admitted to the Union between 1791 and 1803. The vast and sparsely settled Indiana Territory was across the western borders of Kentucky and Ohio and, farther west still, across the Mississippi, was France's Louisiana Territory, which would be sold to the United States in 1803 for $15,000,000. By shortly after midcentury, momentous changes had occurred. To the seventeen states which existed in 1803, fourteen new ones had been added: Maine, Florida, Alabama, Mississippi, Louisiana, Arkansas, Missouri, Michigan, Wisconsin, Iowa, Illinois, Indiana, Texas, and California. With those areas not yet admitted to statehood established as territories, the final configuration of the first 48 states was not far from being resolved. By the year 1900, only three territories in the continental United States were still awaiting statehood—New Mexico, Arizona, and Oklahoma. The end of the nineteenth century represents also the end of the American frontier. The continual westward push of the frontier throughout the history of America up to that point has often been described as its most important characteristic, the component that gave America its distinctive quality. Few could doubt that the century which had seen the frontier closed had produced another, different kind of nation.

At the time of America's first census, in 1790, the population of the country was 3.9 million. By 1880 it had reached 50 million, and then gained 50 percent again in the next 20 years to reach 76 million by the end of the century. This vast population growth had not been reached just through births in America. The nineteenth century was the century of immigration—nine million immigrants came to America between 1880 and 1900 alone—in the United States, the great majority coming from northern and western Europe. Only in the last years of the century was there a fundamental shift with the majority beginning to come from southern and eastern Europe. With the closing of the frontier and the vast increases in immigration came two other fundamental shifts—the growth of America as an increasingly urban nation, and the rise of modern industrial society.

At the start of the nineteenth century, America was still rural. As the Industrial Revolution took hold, manufacturing industries grew and with them urban centers. By 1880, the Bureau of the Census calculated that 28 percent of Americans lived in urban areas; by 1900 that figure had reached 40 percent. In industry also, the last two decades of the century produced the most startling growth up to that time. Steel production went from 1.4 million tons in 1880 to 11 million tons in 1900, a period in which the aggregate annual value of all manufactured goods in America almost tripled. The nineteenth century was an age of innovation and invention in every area; transportation was transformed by the steamboat and the railroad, and at the end of the century, the automobile made its debut. Communication was transformed by the telegraph, the typewriter, photography, the telephone, the Linotype, and other inventions. Daily life was radically changed by electric lighting; manufacturing processes of every kind were revolutionized. With industry and the urbanization of America came new kinds of problems, of housing, disease, crime, conflicts between cultures thrown close together, and conflicts between business and labor. The first effective American labor organization that was national in scope, the Knights of Labor, was organized in 1869 and reached its peak in 1885 with a membership of almost 700,000. Strikes were common, often aimed at preventing reductions in wages; the eight-hour day was an unattained goal. Violence perpetrated by anarchists during the 1886 Haymarket Riot in Chicago cost labor both public support and membership. Union participation didn't reach its 1885–86 levels again until the year 1900.

Viewed from our perspective, the Civil War stands across the 19th century as the Great Divide, the cataclysm into which the young nation was thrust less than a century after it was founded and from which it emerged four years later, badly battered, into the modern world. Slavery had become a part of American society very early. In 1670, there may have been 2,000 slaves in Virginia; fifty years later, perhaps ten times that many. By the Revolution, there were 150,000 slaves in Virginia with corresponding numbers in other southern states. The tobacco, sugar, and cotton industries were ideally suited to plantations, where slavery flourished long after it had been banished from the North. It has been calculated that in 1850 only a few hundred thousand of the six million whites in the slave states owned any slaves at all, and that fewer than 2,000 owned a hundred or more. In the Civil War the entire region rose to defend a way of life which was enjoyed at its peak by only a few.

For decades before the Civil War the country was split by controversy over whether slavery should be allowed in new states and territories. Abraham Lincoln came to prominence in Illinois in the 1850s campaigning against the Kansas-Nebraska Act of 1854, the creation of his political rival Stephen A. Douglas, which established the principle that the citizens of each new territory would decide the question of slavery within their borders themselves. In practical terms, this plan was unworkable because it only served to make each new territory a battleground, as Kansas became a particularly violent battleground in 1855–56. Lincoln opposed the Kansas-Nebraska Act on philosophical grounds; in those years, his position was that slavery should be restricted to the old South, where it had always existed, in the hope that, if contained, it might one day die out. Reaction to the Supreme Court's decision in the Dred Scott case in 1857 served to further polarize the nation. In the Dred Scott case, Chief Justice Roger Taney had found that the federal government could not constitutionally bar slavery in new territories. In this atmosphere of unremitting debate and great tension, the southern states began to think, not for the first time, of secession from a Union which might no longer represent their interests. Lincoln's election in November, 1860 was the signal that the time for secession was at hand. South Carolina led the way on December 20, soon to be followed by the other states, which established a Confederate government with Jefferson Davis as President even before Lincoln could be inaugurated in Washington the following March. The next month, when the Confederates opened fire on Fort Sumter in Charleston harbor, the war—for Lincoln, the war to save the Union—was on.

The Union began the Civil War with advantages over the Confederacy. It had more than twice the population—just over 20 million to nine million in the Confederate states. The Union had over a million industrial workers, the Confederacy a hundred thousand. The Union contained over seventy percent of the nation's 30,000 miles of railroad tracks. Despite these disadvantages, the Confederate Army scored major victories early in the war at Bull Run, Fredericksburg, and elsewhere. The tide turned in 1863 at Gettysburg and Vicksburg, and the Union pressed their advantage in 1864 with Grant in Virginia and Sherman in the deep South. After evacuating Richmond in April, 1865, Lee had no choice but to surrender on Union terms. The war which began to save the Union had ended by freeing the slaves after all. Lincoln had announced the Emancipation Proclamation in September, 1862, to be effective the following January. By that time freeing the slaves in the Confederate states had come to be viewed as a military necessity. Emancipation would be praised in Europe— Lincoln always feared that foreign nations might recognize the Confederate government and thereby involve the Union in an international conflict while it still had the rebels at home to contend with. Emancipation would deprive the Confederacy of a part of their domestic work force and would provide recruits for the North—before the end of the war almost 200,000 blacks had served in Federal armies. After the Civil War was over, and Lincoln was dead, slavery was formally abolished in the United States by constitutional amendment; this proved to be the beginning, not the end, of the struggle for racial equality in America.

■ The first **New York Stock Exchange** *(left)*, which opened in 1792. This early illustration shows a few of the 24 merchants and brokers who organized the exchange—only a year after the country's first such exchange was established in Philadelphia—doing business at their favorite spot, under a button-weed tree on New York's Wall Street.

■ **Eli Whitney** *(bottom left)* in his workshop. The Massachusetts-born inventor revolutionized agriculture in the South with his cotton gin, patented in 1795. The device made it possible to remove seeds from cotton cheaply and quickly, thereby making cotton a much more profitable crop.

■ A scene from the 1807 trial of former Vice-President **Aaron Burr** *(bottom center)*, acquitted on this occasion by the Circuit Court of the district of Virginia. Burr, who in 1804 had killed his political rival Alexander Hamilton in a duel, had been indicted for treason because of his involvement in vaguely defined plots to form a separate country in the southwestern part of the United States.

■ **Benjamin Franklin** *(bottom right)*, from a painting by Charles Willson Peale. As a printer, publisher, inventor—of bifocals and the lightning rod, among other things—Franklin had a tremendous impact on American life in Pennsylvania and the other colonies during the last half of the 18th century. He provided a statesmanlike presence at the Second Continental Congress and at the Constitutional Convention of 1787; his services to the new Republic included long years as a diplomat in France where he worked to secure military and financial assistance for the new nation during the Revolution.

■ This lithograph published by Root and Tinker in New York in 1885 commemorates the life of **Noah Webster** *(top),* showing his early *Spelling Book* (1783), a page of his manuscript, the title page of the first version of his dictionary, the *Compendious Dictionary of the English Language* (1806), and a late 19th-century edition of his *American Dictionary of the English Language,* first published in 1828. A schoolteacher educated at Yale, Webster was dissatisfied with the reference books of his day which, originating in England, ignored American culture. The success of his own made his name synonymous with dictionaries for generations of Americans.

■ An N.C. Wyeth painting of the Shoshone woman **Sacajawea** *(bottom),* helping guide the expedition of Captains Meriwether Lewis and William Clark on their epic 4,000 mile journey to the Pacific Northwest in 1804–1806. Captured by Indian enemies of her tribe when she was a child, Sacajawea was eventually sold to a French-Canadian fur trader, Toussaint Charbonneau. When Charbonneau was hired to accompany Lewis and Clark as an interpreter, Sacajawea and her infant son joined the explorers and their 26-man party. Sacajawea proved a valuable guide in the unexplored wilderness and assisted in negotiations with the Shoshones for horses needed to cross the Rocky Mountains. The Lewis and Clark expedition reached the Pacific at the mouth of the Columbia River in November, 1805, and the following year they made their way back to the East, arriving in St. Louis in September, 1806. Their account of the journey is one of the classics of American travel literature.

■ **The Battle of Tippecanoe** *(top)* in an 1889 Kurz and Allison lithograph of the counterattack commanded by William Henry Harrison, Governor of the Indiana Territory and a captain in the regular army, against the Shawnee Indians led by Tecumseh and his brother The Prophet. Harrison and his troop of 1,000 men had marched 150 miles north from Vincennes to attack the Indian encampment at the junction of Tippecanoe Creek and the Wabash River, which they reached on November 6, 1811. The following morning the Indians attacked Harrison's camp and were turned back only after a day-long struggle; the next day Harrison's men destroyed the Indian village. In the long conflict caused by the pressure of westward-moving settlement, the Shawnees made at Tippecanoe one of their last stands against incursion on their historic native land, and the power of their great leader Tecumseh was broken in the struggle. British support of the Shawnees was one of the causes of the War of 1812.

■ The War of 1812 was a sidelight to the final phase of the long struggle between Napoleonic France and Great Britain. The conflict was primarily caused by the British practice of boarding American ships to seize or "impress" American sailors—some of whom were indeed deserters from the British Navy—and by British attempts to blockade French ports to American shipping. The rather inconclusive military action began with a Declaration of War signed by President James Madison on June 18, 1812, and ended with the Treaty of Ghent on December 24, 1814. Though the war accomplished relatively little, individual episodes quickly became part of the folklore of the new nation. A legendary American naval victory of the War of 1812 occurred on August 19, 1812 in the north Atlantic when the American frigate **Constitution** *(middle)* outgunned the British warship *Guerrière.* As shown in this lithograph, the ships fired at each other at close range until the more heavily armed American frigate under the command of Captain Isaac Hull destroyed the *Guerrière's* masts and rigging.

■ An historic moment in **The Battle of Lake Erie** *(bottom),* from a painting by Percy Moran. On September 10, 1813, the commander of the small American fleet on Lake Erie, Oliver Hazard Perry, engaged the British from his flagship, the *Lawrence.* When the *Lawrence* was crippled, Perry was rowed under heavy fire to the *Niagara* from which he continued the fight. After heavy losses on both sides, the *Niagara* was able to break through the British defenses and destroy two key enemy ships, the *Detroit* and the *Queen Charlotte.* Late in the day the remainder of the British fleet surrendered, and Perry sent his famous message to William Henry Harrison, "We have met the enemy and they are ours." Following this defeat, the British had no choice but to evacuate their ground troops from Detroit.

■ Major General **Andrew Jackson** *(above),* commander of the American forces at the Battle of New Orleans. The defeat suffered by the British at New Orleans in the early days of January, 1815 both marked the end of the War of 1812 and stimulated the rise of the Jackson legend which would carry him to the Presidency in the following decade. After the battle, which cost them 2,100 lives, the British learned that the war was already over, the peace treaty having been signed in Europe two weeks earlier.

■ As the conflict was winding down in September, 1814, the British army, having burned Washington, attacked the city of Baltimore. Stalled on land, the British called for naval reinforcements and a British fleet positioned itself to bombard Fort McHenry at the mouth of the harbor. **Francis Scott Key** *(right),* a Baltimore attorney, boarded the British ship, the *Minden,* with two companions, to negotiate the release of an American prisoner. The release was arranged after a cordial dinner with the British officers, who decided, however, to hold the American contingent until after their attack on Fort McHenry. So, on the evening of September 14, Key and his friends watched through the night from the deck of the *Minden* as the British shelled the fort. In the morning the fort was still standing, still in American hands, and the huge flag—42 by 30 feet—which had stood over it all night was still flying. Moved by the occasion, Key wrote the words to *The Star Spangled Bannner* which in 1931 was declared by law the national anthem. This later nineteenth-century print presents an idealized view of Key on the British ship watching the flag over Fort McHenry.

■ A draft of the final version of **The Star Spangled Banner** *(below)* in the handwriting of Francis Scott Key. The tune was that of a British drinking song which dated from at least Colonial times and had been used after the Revolution with other patriotic lyrics.

■ President **James Monroe** *(left)* in a painting by Chappell. Elected President in 1816 and reelected in 1820, Monroe governed during the so-called "Era of Good Feelings," a time of national confidence, freedom from foreign wars, and economic expansion. Toward the end of his second administration he spelled out the Monroe Doctrine, the concept that the United States must oppose any attempt by European nations to interfere in the politics of the Western Hemisphere.

■ A photograph of **Edgar Allan Poe** *(left, middle)* taken in 1848 at Providence, Rhode Island. A year later, on October 7, 1849, Poe died in Baltimore at the age of 40. An American original, Poe cultivated a sense of the mysterious and macabre in poems such as *The Raven* (1845) and short stories like *The Murders In the Rue Morgue* (1841).

". . . no, never need an American look beyond his own country for the sublime and beautiful of natural scenery."

—WASHINGTON IRVING

■ **Washington Irving** *(left),* often described as the first American man of letters, the first American author to have an international reputation. In his classic short stories, *The Legend of Sleepy Hollow* and *Rip Van Winkle,* first published in 1820, he created some of the enduring characters of early American fiction.

■ Lockport, New York on the **Erie Canal** *(above),* a lithograph by J.H. Bufford after a drawing by W. Wilson. Sponsored by New York Governor DeWitt Clinton, and built between 1817 and 1825 at a cost of $7,000,000, the Erie Canal, stretching 363 miles from Buffalo, New York to Albany, helped open to settlers from the East vast territories in what later became the states of Michigan, Ohio, Indiana, and Illinois. Connecting with the Hudson River near Albany, the canal made it possible for farm produce to be shipped quickly and easily to the East to be marketed, and made it equally possible for freight and manufactured goods to be shipped west. The Erie Canal paid for itself within a few years. Seen in this view are a few of the 82 locks needed to surmount the 500-foot rise in elevation west of Troy, New York.

■ Naturalist **John James Audubon** *(above),* whose *Birds of America,* published in London in 1827–38 in four folio volumes with 453 hand-colored plates illustrating all known species of North American birds, was one of the first scientific classics created by an American and a landmark of ornithological art.

■ **Davy Crockett** *(below),* Indian fighter in the Creek War 1813–15, frontiersman, politician who represented Tennessee in Congress several times in the 1820s and 1830s, and martyr at the Alamo in 1836 at the age of 50. More complex than the untutored woodsman portrayed by Disney in the 1950s, Crockett adroitly used the backwoods legends about himself to political advantage; he told part of his true story in his *Autobiography* written with Thomas Chilton and published in 1834.

■ **Defenders of the Alamo** *(above),* an episode of the mid-1830s struggle which established the independence of Texas from Mexico. By 1830 American settlers in Texas outnumbered Mexicans four to one though the area was nominally part of Mexico, which had gained its own independence from Spain only in 1821. In November, 1835, the Texas settlers established a provisional government of their own and named Sam Houston commander of their army. War with Mexico followed. The Texans suffered a reverse in the battle for San Antonio in February-March, 1836 when 200 volunteers perished at the Alamo, an 18th-century Franciscan mission. The dead included Col. James Bowie and legendary frontiersman Davy Crockett, as the small force of Texans was unable to withstand the 4,000-man army of Mexican General Antonio López de Santa Anna. Only six weeks after the fall of the Alamo, the tide was turned when Sam Houston's forces surprised and defeated Santa Anna's army at San Jacinto, thus securing the independence of Texas. Houston was elected first President of the Republic of Texas, and in 1845 he brought Texas into the United States.

■ This **daguerreotype from the Mexican
War** *(left)*, 1846–48, one of the first war photographs ever taken, shows American officers on
horseback in Saltillo. Hostilities began over the
annexation of Texas by the United States in 1845
and ended when Mexico City fell to American
troops on September 14, 1847. By the terms of
the peace treaty, the United States acquired for
$15,000,000 virtually all the territory compris-
ing the present states of Arizona, New Mexico,
Utah, Nevada, and California.

■ **Stephen Foster** *(below)*, photographed not
long before his death in 1864 in New York City.
During his short active life—unappreciated in
his time, he died in poverty at the age of 37—
he wrote about 200 songs, many of them American classics such as "Oh, Susanna", "Old Folks
At Home", "Camptown Races", and "Jeanie With
the Light Brown Hair". Though often thought of
as a southerner because of the minstrel-song
nature of his music, Foster was born near Pittsburgh, lived in the North, and made only one
brief trip to the South in 1852.

■ **Samuel F.B. Morse** *(below)*, demonstrating
his revolutionary invention, the telegraph. After
graduating from Yale in 1810, Morse studied art
in England, and returned to the United States in
1815 to work as a portrait painter. A founder of
the National Academy of Design, Morse served
as its first president, 1826–45. He produced his
first working model of the telegraph in 1835,
and later developed the code which bears his
name.

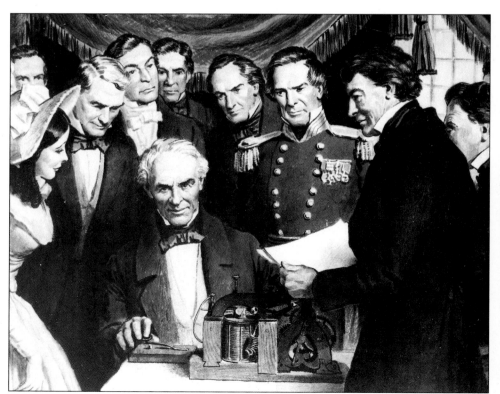

■ **The California Gold Rush** of 1849 brought miners such as these *(top, left)* to river beds throughout the northern part of the state. The Gold Rush had its origin on January 24, 1848 when James Marshall, a carpenter from New Jersey, found gold in the American river at Coloma, 50 miles from Sacramento, where he was building a saw mill for a Californian named John Sutter. The rush started quietly, but was going full blast by the summer of 1849—possibly 80,000 people headed west before the end of that year, some by ship around the tip of South America, but most of them overland from every inhabited part of the country. The three prospectors shown here panning for gold in a river bed, as was done by thousands during the original Gold Rush, were photographed in the Dakotas in 1889.

■ **A wagon train** *(top, right)* which didn't make it to Pike's Peak in Colorado in the years after the first Gold Rush. For the rest of the century after 1849, rumors of new strikes—some genuine, most not—brought fortune-seekers rushing to almost every part of the Old West at one time or another.

■ **An advertisement** *(left)* for a ship offering to take prospective miners to California—speed was definitely an inducement.

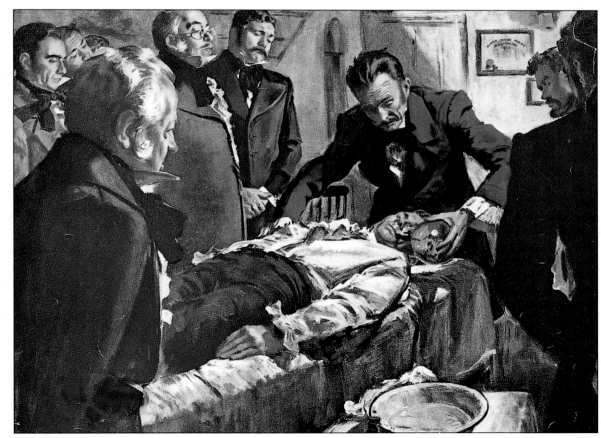

■ **The first operation performed with a general anesthetic** *(right)* was the removal of a facial tumor at Massachusetts General Hospital in Boston, October 16, 1846, accomplished with the help of ether gas, the invention of a Boston dentist, Dr. William T.G. Morton.

■ *Fur Traders Descending the Missouri*, George Caleb Bingham's classic painting *(above)*. Much of the American West was first explored by fur traders whose ranks included such legendary figures as Jim Bridger and Kit Carson. For the fur trader, the Missouri was the route to the Pacific Northwest. They followed it upstream to the richest trapping country and brought their pelts back down it to trade. One of the first major industries in the new republic, the trade in fur flourished through the first decades of the 19th century and then declined as fashions changed and fur-bearing animals became more scarce.

■ **An 1851 Boston placard** *(right)* warns blacks, escaped slaves and others, to be wary of the agents of the fugitive slave laws out for rewards for returned slaves. During the years of the Underground Railroad, a movement that began with the Quakers of Pennsylvania in the 18th century, opponents of slavery developed a massive network of refuges for escaped slaves, and helped many thousands find freedom in the North.

UNCLE TOM'S CABIN

ELIZA'S ESCAPE

■ A 19th-century theatrical poster for the stage version of **Uncle Tom's Cabin** *(left)*. Few works of fiction ever struck such a responsive chord as Harriet Beecher Stowe's novel, serialized in the anti-slavery *National Era* in 1851 and published in book form the following year. Hundreds of thousands of copies were sold within a few months, and the play, adapted from Stowe's novel without her consent, appeared almost immediately and became a staple of American popular drama.

■ **Emily Dickinson** *(below),* the reclusive poet of Amherst, Massachusetts who published only a handful of her 800 poems during her lifetime, but whose reputation as a master of short, lyric verse has soared in this century.

■ **John Brown** *(below),* militant white Abolitionist who became involved in anti-slavery violence in Kansas in the mid-1850s. He later formulated the idea of establishing a secure area for escaped blacks in Virginia and Maryland. Toward that end, he led a band of sixteen whites and five blacks, who seized the Federal armory at Harper's Ferry, Virginia on October 16, 1859, taking a number of hostages in the process. He held out for a day but was overpowered by a detachment of marines. Brown was tried for murder, slave insurrection, and treason, convicted and executed; in death he was widely revered as a heroic martyr of the Abolitionist movement.

■ **Sojourner Truth** *(opposite, bottom right),* a major figure in the struggle for the rights of blacks and women in the 19th century. Born a slave in New York State in 1797, she took, as Isabella Van Wagener, the surname of the master who set her free in 1827 just before New York State abolished slavery. In the 1840s she became under the name Sojourner Truth an itinerant black evangelist who preached not only the goodness of God but the gospel of Abolitionism. Her magnetic personality drew large crowds throughout the northern states; she supported herself by selling copies of the autobiography, *The Narrative of Sojourner Truth,* which she dictated, never having learned to read and write. Before the Civil War, she added women's suffrage to the causes she supported, and during the war years raised supplies for black regiments. She continued to lecture and work for civil rights for blacks and women until her death in 1883.

"We never know how high we are
Till we are called to rise
And then, if we are true to plan
Our statures touch the skies."

—EMILY DICKINSON

■ **Wall Street during the Panic of 1857** *(top),* a lithograph by Cafferty and Rosenberg. Overspeculation in railroad stocks and real estate, and the failure of the New York branch of the huge Ohio Life Insurance and Trust Company, caused the dramatic panic which saw investors rushing to remove funds from banks before withdrawals could be suspended. Across the nation, several thousand companies failed.

■ **A Pony Express Rider** *(bottom),* heading for St. Joseph, Missouri during the brief period from April, 1860 until October, 1861 when the Pony Express attempted to supply continuous mail delivery between St. Joseph and Sacramento, California. There were 157 stations on the 1,800 mile route; it took about ten days for a letter to cross the country this unique way with riders stopping frequently to change horses. Running the service was too expensive to be profitable, and it ceased when the transcontinental telegraph was completed, but it did make legends out of some of its more colorful riders, including William "Buffalo Bill" Cody.

■ **Abraham Lincoln** *(above left),* six-teenth President of the United States, elected in 1860 when the conflict over slavery was at its height and the crisis brought about by the southern states' plan to secede from the Union was at hand. Lincoln was opposed to slavery on philosophical grounds, but at the start of the Civil War he considered the preservation of the Union the main issue. In 1863, he freed the slaves as a necessary military and political measure. His 1865 second inaugural address was a call for conciliation with the South as the war was winding down and the victory of the North was assured. Lincoln was shot by John Wilkes Booth on April 14, 1865, before his plans for the reconstructed country could be implemented; he died the following day.

■ **The Lincoln-Douglas Debates** *(above right)* of 1858 brought Lincoln to national prominence as spokesman for the Republican Party. In the series of seven debates during the Illinois Senatorial race against Democrat Stephen A. Douglas, Lincoln elaborated his opposition to slavery and to allowing it to spread to new states and territories. Douglas won the close election, but Lincoln's eloquence helped him claim the Republican presidential nomination two years later.

■ **The inauguration of Jefferson Davis** *(right)* as President of the Confederacy at a convention at Montgomery, Alabama in February, 1861. A few months later the Confederate capital was moved to Richmond, Virginia. Davis served as President of the Confederate States of America throughout its existence. During a futile effort to continue the struggle after Lee's surrender in 1865, Davis was captured by Union forces near Irwinville, Georgia on May 10, 1865, and was imprisoned for two years. A charge of treason against him was not prosecuted. He died in 1889.

■ *Stonewall Jackson at Bull Run (above)*, a painting by H. A. Ogden. The Civil War began with the Confederates firing on Fort Sumter in Charleston harbor on April 12, 1861. The Union immediately began both to blockade southern ports and to assemble a volunteer army. The First Battle of Bull Run near Manassas Junction in northern Virginia was the earliest major ground action of the war. At a crucial point the brigade led by then Col. Thomas Jackson held firm in the face of a Union assault, and one of the Confederate generals gave Jackson the nickname by which he has been known ever since. The 34,000-man Union Army, somewhat larger than the Confederate force, but inexperienced and poorly led, was turned back in its attempt to reach the Confederate capital at Richmond. The Confederates brought some of their troops to the battle area by train—the first strategic use of rail transportation in the history of warfare.

■ **The Union ironclad *Monitor* battles the Confederates' *Merrimac*** *(right, top)* off Hampton Roads, Virginia on March 9, 1862. The *Merrimac* had inflicted considerable damage on the Union fleet on March 8, before the *Monitor* arrived, but the battle between the two ironclads was inconclusive. The *Merrimac* was actually a refitted frigate which the Confederates called the *Virginia*, but the *Monitor* had been designed and built as an ironclad. The careers of these two unusual ships were destined to be short. The Confederates destroyed the *Merrimac (Virginia)* when they evacuated Norfolk in May, 1862, and later that year the *Monitor* sank in a gale off Cape Hatteras, North Carolina.

■ **The Battle of Fredericksburg** *(right, bottom)* in Virginia on December 13, 1862 was a devastating defeat for the Union forces. In this engraving, Union soldiers are building a pontoon bridge across the 400-foot wide Rappahannock River. The more than three weeks it took to construct the bridge gave the Confederate forces time to build up their strength. The Union Army under General Ambrose Burnside, who had relieved McClellan, was repulsed, and Burnside was soon replaced by General Joseph Hooker. Lincoln was still looking for the generals who would bring victory over Lee.

■ **Lincoln and McClellan** *(opposite)*, meeting after the Battle of Antietam, in a famous photograph by Alexander Gardner. The Union Army under McClellan halted Lee's advance on Washington at the Battle of Antietam near Sharpsburg, Maryland on September 17, 1862. Over 25,000 Union and Confederate casualties, including almost 5,000 killed, made Antietam the bloodiest single day of the war, but McClellan missed an opportunity to smash the Confederate Army decisively. In early November, McClellan was fired for the indecision which Lincoln believed had cost the Union a more impressive victory. The victory at Antietam was important enough, however, for Lincoln to take the opportunity a few days afterward to announce the Emancipation Proclamation, to go into effect the following January 1, freeing the slaves in the Confederate states.

■ **A soldier of the Civil War** *(right)* dead on the battlefield. Though the data are incomplete, battle deaths in the Civil War totaled over 270,000—140,414 confirmed on the Union side, 133,821 from the Confederacy—almost as many as in World War II, and far more than in any other American war. Tens of thousands more died of disease in hospitals and prison camps on both sides.

■ **Pickett's Charge** *(below left)* at the Battle of Gettysburg. In this desperate attempt, ordered by Lee on the battle's third day, the division commanded by General George Pickett attempted to storm the center of the Union position. When the assault failed, with thousands of casualties, the tide of the war had turned.

■ **James Ewell Brown "Jeb" Stuart** *(below right),* Confederate cavalry officer. In the first year of the Civil War, Stuart was given command of the cavalry brigade of the Army of Northern Virginia, and was so successful in providing accurate intelligence to the Confederate command that Robert E. Lee once called him the "eyes of the army." Having served brilliantly in the defense of Richmond in June, 1862, at the Second Battle of Bull Run, and at the Battle of Fredericksburg, Stuart took command of the Confederate 2nd Army Corps at the Battle of Chancellorsville in May, 1863 after Stonewall Jackson had been wounded. At the Battle of Gettysburg, however, Stuart earned the criticism of later strategists by being caught out of position on a raid and unable to join Lee at the crucial time. Stuart was killed in action at Yellow Tavern, near Richmond, Virginia— part of the Battle of Spotsylvania—on May 12, 1864.

■ **Mathew Brady** *(right),* the leading photographic portrait artist of his day, went on to become the most famous Civil War photographer. He set out for Bull Run with his camera at the start of the war and continued actively until the end. Several pioneer American photographers who are now famous in their own right—A.J. Russell, T.H. O'Sullivan, and Alexander Gardner—worked for Brady during the Civil War years. The portrait of Brady was made on July 22, 1861, after his return to Washington from the Battle of Bull Run.

> *"Whatever there is of greatness in the United States, or indeed in any other country, is due to labor. The laborer is the author of all the greatness and wealth. Without labor there would be no government, and no leading class, and nothing to preserve."*
>
> —ULYSSES S. GRANT

■ **Union artillery in action** *(above).* The lenses of the cumbersome wetplate cameras of the Civil War period were far too slow to 'freeze' battle action. This slightly blurred photograph is one of the rare prints actually made during a Civil War engagement. Probably photographed by Timothy O'Sullivan, it shows Battery 'D' of the fifth United States Artillery in action at Fredericksburg, Virginia on May 3, 1863.

■ **General Ulysses S. Grant** *(right)* in a Brady photograph taken before the battle of Spotsylvania, Virginia in May, 1864. A native of Ohio, Grant had served in the Mexican War in the 1840s. He resigned from the Army in 1854, partly because of warnings from superior officers about his well-known drinking habits. After he rejoined the Army at the start of the Civil War, Grant's successes, culminating in the taking of Vicksburg, Mississippi in 1863, brought him command of all Union armies. He proved to be the leader that Lincoln had been looking for since the war began, and presided over the campaigns that led to victory in 1865. His two terms as President, 1869–1877, were marred by corruption scandals involving close associates. He died in 1885; his posthumous *Personal Memoirs* became a classic of American political literature.

■ **The ruins of Richmond, Virginia**
(above), the capital of the Confederacy, in the last days of the Civil War. Richmond and Petersburg, Virginia, were occupied by Union troops on April 4, 1865, after a long siege. When it was over, Lee's army was finished and the end of the war was inevitable. Lincoln, restless in Washington waiting for news, toured the ruins of Richmond in the last days before Lee's surrender, and found the city devastated, many buildings having been set on fire by retreating Confederate soldiers. As the remaining white citizens of Richmond watched from behind closed curtains, crowds of blacks, now finally free, mobbed Lincoln and his son Tad as they walked through the streets of the smouldering city.

■ **General Robert E. Lee** *(right)* seated at left, facing Grant and his officers as he signed the surrender document in the front parlor of a house owned by Wilmer McLean at Appomattox Courthouse, Virginia on April 9, 1865. Lee's 27,000-man army had no chance of escape following the fall of Richmond a few days earlier. The North had a million men in uniform at that time, the Confederacy not even a hundred thousand. McLean had lived near Manassas Junction at the start of the war and a shell passed through his house during the first Battle of Bull Run, sometime after which he moved to Appomattox. In later years he was fond of saying that the Civil War had started in his back yard and ended in his parlor. Grant, who had written to Lee on April 7 urging him to surrender and avoid further bloodshed, proposed terms which the Confederates thought generous. Officers were free to keep their side arms and personal possessions. Those officers and men who owned their own horses were free to keep them, and all were free to return to their homes.

■ **The assassination of Lincoln** *(below),* an engraving recreating the scene at Ford's Theatre in Washington as actor John Wilkes Booth shot Lincoln in the back of the head during the third act of a popular comedy, *Our American Cousin.* The murder of Lincoln on April 14, 1865, only five days after Lee's surrender, was the culmination of plans which Booth had been developing for years. Unable to kidnap Lincoln, his original intention, Booth and his fellow conspirators changed their plans to the assassination of Lincoln and other members of the federal government. Secretary of State William Seward was stabbed and badly wounded by one of Booth's accomplices, Lewis T. Paine, but survived. Another accomplice, George Atzerodt, had been too frightened to carry out his task, the killing of Vice President Andrew Johnson. Though he broke a bone in his leg swinging himself down to the stage after shooting Lincoln, Booth escaped to nearby Virginia and eluded a massive manhunt for twelve days. Surrounded by Federal troops in a barn on a farm just south of the Rappahannock River, Booth either shot himself or was shot by a soldier.

■ A photographic portrait of **Jesse James** *(left)* at the age of 17 in 1864, when he was fighting for the Confederacy as a member of "Bloody" Bill Anderson's guerrilla troop on the western frontier. Shot and wounded by Federal troops at the end of the war, James turned to the life of crime which would make his name a legend throughout the Old West. Beginning with robbing banks, stagecoaches and stores, in the 1870s James and his gang added hijacking trains to their repertoire. One of their more famous episodes was the raid on the First National Bank of Northfield, Minnesota on September 7, 1876, when of the eight-member gang only Jesse and his brother Frank escaped being killed or captured. Jesse was killed by one of his gang's members, Robert Ford, in 1882 for the $10,000 reward being offered by Missouri Governor Thomas T. Crittenden.

■ Actor **John Wilkes Booth** *(left),* son of one famous actor, Junius Brutus Booth, and brother of Edwin Booth, the most celebrated actor of his day. A passionate defender of the Southern cause, Booth performed on stage throughout the South during the Civil War, while serving off and on as a Confederate agent. Though many voiced their suspicions after the assassination, no credible evidence has ever surfaced linking Booth's plot with Jefferson Davis and the Confederate leadership.

■ **The execution by hanging** *(above)* of four of Booth's co-conspirators on the Arsenal grounds of Washington's Old Penitentiary Building on July 7, 1865. Four others were sentenced to terms of imprisonment. Those hanged were Paine, Atzerodt, Mary Surratt, and David Herold. Surratt ran a boardinghouse where Booth's group sometimes met; Herold had been with Booth when Booth died. This photograph shows a large group on the scaffold moments before General Winfield Scott Hancock gave the order for the hanging; the condemned prisoners are being shielded from the sun with umbrellas.

■ Secretary of the Interior **William Seward** *(above left)* explaining his plans to purchase Alaska from Russia. Though he was ridiculed at the time—"Seward's Folly" was considered a useless wasteland—history proved Seward astute and pragmatic. The $7,200,000 purchase price worked out to about two cents an acre; even so, the Senate vote approving the purchase on April 9, 1867 barely passed.

■ **John Wesley Powell** and his exploring party *(above)*. Powell, the figure kneeling at left, led a series of expeditions which surveyed the Green and Colorado River canyons in the 1870s; these led to the publication of his classic account, *Exploration of the Colorado River of the West and Its Tributaries* (1875), revised as *Canyons of Colorado* in 1895. A pioneering student of Indian languages, Powell headed the U.S. Bureau of Ethnology of the Smithsonian Institution from its establishment in 1879 until his death in 1902.

■ **Herman Melville** *(left, middle),* a giant of 19th-century American literature whose masterpiece, *Moby Dick,* barely stirred a critical ripple when published in 1851. Melville went to sea in the 1830s and drew on his experiences for many of his books, including *Typee* (1846) and *Omoo* (1847). A commercial failure as an author, Melville was a customs inspector on the New York waterfront after 1866. By the time Melville died in 1891, it had been decades since any of his books had been published; one factor in the rise of his reputation in this century was the discovery and publication of his short novel *Billy Budd* in 1924.

■ **Louisa May Alcott** *(left, bottom).* Daughter of New England religious visionary Bronson Alcott, Louisa May grew up in the rarefied intellectual atmosphere of Boston in the age of Emerson and Thoreau. A nurse during the Civil War, she turned to writing to support the family for which her unpractical father could not adequately provide. After a book of fairy stories, *Flower Fables* (1854), and another on her wartime experiences, *Hospital Sketches* (1863), her literary career blossomed with *Little Women,* serialized in the *Atlantic Monthly* in 1868–69, and published in book form to wide acclaim. Alcott had not only achieved financial security, but discovered her métier; other well-received children's books, and some more serious novels, followed. She died in 1888.

> *"The other world beyond this, which was longed for by the devout before Columbus's time, was found in the New; and the deep-sea lead, that first struck these soundings, brought up the soil of Earth's Paradise."*
>
> —HERMAN MELVILLE

■ Workmen celebrating the completion of the **first transcontinental railroad** *(above)* at Promontory, Utah, seventy miles northwest of Salt Lake City, on May 10, 1869. At Promontory, the new track laid east from Sacramento, California by the Central Pacific Railroad joined track laid west from Omaha, Nebraska by the Union Pacific. In the background, the two locomotives, the Central Pacific's *Jupiter* (left), and the Union Pacific's *No. 119,* are facing each other while in front, the Central Pacific's Samuel S. Montague shakes hands with the Union Pacific's Grenville M. Dodge. The 1,776 miles of track between Sacramento and Omaha were completed ahead of schedule, using only man and animal power, following passage of the Pacific Railroad Act of 1864. The two railroads raced each other relentlessly, as each mile finished entitled them to lucrative government land grants and loan bonds. In this competitive frenzy, it seemed possible that they would each keep laying tracks and never meet, but under pressure from the federal government, Promontory was selected as the juncture. On the final day, Leland Stanford, president of the Central Pacific, tried with a silver-headed maul to drive the ceremonial golden last spike into a special tie of laurel wood, but swung and missed. Stanford passed the maul to the Union Pacific's Thomas Durant who politely missed also. Somehow, the spike was driven, and workmen rushed to replace the laurel tie and golden spike with standard equipment, as a telegrapher on the scene sent the simple message 'Done,' setting off celebrations from coast to coast. When the transcontinental railroad was completed, it was barely more than 40 years since the first American railroad, the Baltimore and Ohio Company, had received its charter on February 28, 1827. In 1830 the B and O began operating on its first 13 miles of track between Baltimore and Ellicott's Mills, Maryland. In the 19th century, railroads spread quickly. By 1840 there were 2,800 miles of track in the United States, 30,000 miles by the start of the Civil War. The westward thrust of railroad construction continued at a hectic pace even after 1869 as more and more networks of track shortened distances between parts of the country that a few decades earlier had been separated by oceans of prairie and forbidding mountains. Nothing could have symbolized more clearly than this photograph the inevitable closing of the American frontier.

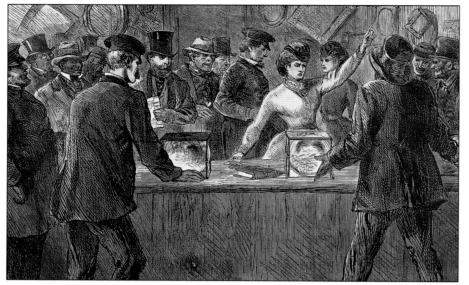

■ **Victoria Woodhull** *(top)* in a contemporary engraving, asserting, to no avail, her right to vote. Woodhull packed an enormous amount into her long life. Advocate of women's suffrage, for which she argued before a Congressional committee after the Civil War, she also espoused at different times free love, spiritualism, socialism, and various sorts of economic reforms. She was both the first woman to run for President, as a candidate of the Equal Rights Party in 1872—Frederick Douglass was nominated as her running mate, but he declined to run—and the publisher, also in 1872, in her periodical *Woodhull and Claflin's Weekly,* of the first English translation of Marx and Engels's *Communist Manifesto.* In the later 1870s, she moved to London, married a wealthy English banker, and became involved in various philanthropic causes. She published a journal dealing with eugenics, and, in 1914, offered a prize of $5,000 for the first transatlantic airplane flight. She died in 1927 at the age of 88.

■ **The first intercollegiate football game** *(middle),* a painting by W.N. Boyd. Rutgers defeated Princeton by the score of 6 to 4 on November 6, 1869. Princeton won a rematch a week later, 8-0. Four years later Yale, Princeton, Rutgers and Columbia met to draft the first set of standard rules, and by the 1890s college football was a well-established autumn ritual.

■ **Emigrants crossing the Plains** *(bottom),* an engraving by Darley & Hall. Hundreds of thousands went west in the decades after the first wagon trains of the 1840s until the coming of the railroad and the closing of the frontier later in the century. They left each spring from places like Independence, Missouri—groups of families led by experienced guides, often former fur trappers and traders who knew the best routes, where the water was, and how to deal with the Indians. They couldn't leave too early in the year or there wouldn't be grass on the Plains for cattle and oxen to eat; they couldn't leave too late or they risked potential disaster by trying to cross the Rockies after the bad weather set in. Even if things went well it meant a difficult three months or more of fighting the elements, accidents, Indians and boredom, but for many, the covered wagon became a symbol of the desire for freedom and space in the uncharted West.

■ An example of the devastation caused by **the Chicago Fire of 1871** *(above).* Many major American cities had catastrophic fires during the nineteenth century, but none had a bigger one than Chicago. At 9 P.M. on the evening of Sunday, October 8, the fire started in a barn behind Patrick O'Leary's cottage at 137 De Koven Street in a working-class area on the Southwest Side. Whether a cow kicked over a lantern as legend has always had it will never be determined, but there were indeed a cow and a lantern in the O'Leary barn that night. A dry summer and early autumn had left the city, largely built of wood, vulnerable to fires; indeed the Fire Dept., overtaxed from fighting other fires, was slow to respond to the fire on De Koven Street. By 10:30 it was out of control. As the fire grew in the evening and into the night of October 8, a dry hard wind off the prairie to the southwest drove the flames toward the heart of the city. It gathered an unstoppable momentum, and all night and throughout the next day burned virtually everything in a path four miles long and two-thirds of a mile wide. Three hundred people were killed; a hundred thousand, almost a third of the city's population, were left without shelter. As the fire gathered full force, it no longer mattered what the buildings were made of. The wooden shacks and cottages of the poor and the ordinary homes of the middle class went up in flames along with the mansions of the rich, the big hotels, commercial buildings, theaters, the Courthouse where Lincoln had lain-in-state six years before, and the Federal Building, in which—among the documents and records of the Post Office and Customs House—$1,000,000 in currency was burned to ashes. Only a steady rain on the morning of October 10 stopped the flames; by then the famous Gothic Water Tower, which still stands downtown, was the only structure left in the huge burned-out area. Looting was so widespread that federal troops under General Philip Sheridan were called in to take over for the outmanned police. The property damage was estimated at $200,000,000. Despite dire predictions that Chicago had been killed, the city quickly rebuilt itself with Middle Western vigor and enthusiasm. Within a few years Chicago was once again the greatest city west of New York, with only the yellow-stone Water Tower to serve as a reminder of the past before The Fire.

"Men said at vespers: 'All is well!'
In one wild night the city fell;
Fell shrines of prayer and marts of grain
Before the fiery hurricane.

On threescore spires had sunset shone,
Where ghastly sunrise looked on none.
Men clasped each other's hands, and said:
'The city of the West is dead!'"

—JOHN GREENLEAF WHITTIER

■ **Bodies of the dead** *(top left)* litter the ground at the site of the Custer massacre.

■ **A drawing of the Battle of Little Bighorn** *(bottom left)* by an Indian, White Bird.

■ Lieutenant Colonel **George Armstrong Custer** *(below),* 37 years old when he died in the massacre of his Seventh Cavalry troops in the Dakota Territory on June 25, 1876. Custer and 600 soldiers were on a forward mission, detached from the command of General Alfred Terry who was campaigning to force Sioux and Cheyenne Indians onto their reservation. An Indian force, which possibly numbered as many as 3,500 warriors under Chiefs Sitting Bull, Crazy Horse, and Gall, surprised Custer on the banks of the Little Bighorn River after Custer, unaware of the danger at hand, had divided his forces into three groups to patrol separate areas. There were no survivors among Custer's group; in one hour Custer and the 209 men with him were killed along with 53 others in a separate battle a few miles away. This was the worst defeat suffered by the U.S. Army during the Indian Wars.

"*The United States themselves are essentially the greatest poem.*"

—WALT WHITMAN

■ **Martha Jane Cannary** *(left)*, a western original better known as Calamity Jane—Indian scout, sharpshooter, and performer with "Wild Bill" Hickok in his Wild West Show. In the late 1870s she took time out from her adventures to help care for victims of a smallpox epidemic in the Dakota Territory, but whatever she did, she was always in the news.

■ **Alexander Graham Bell** *(bottom left)* at the ceremonial opening of a telephone line between New York and Chicago some years after his 1876 invention of the telephone. Bell was born in Scotland in 1847, and moved with his family to Canada in 1870. He was working in Boston, training teachers of deaf students, when he undertook the scientific work which resulted in the first workable telephone. The first telephone exchange was installed in New Haven, Connecticut in 1877. A decade later there were 150,000 telephones in the United States; a century after that there were over 150,000,000. It has been said that the patent Bell received in March, 1876—Patent #174,465, for a device to transmit speech sounds over electrical wires—was quite possibly the most valuable ever granted.

■ **Walt Whitman** *(bottom right)* in his later life. Poet of the sensual and exuberant *Leaves of Grass,* first published in 1855, and revised and reissued a number of times before his death in 1892, Whitman created an enduring American classic which ran afoul of the censors during its early years—in 1865 Whitman was discharged from his position as a clerk with the U.S. Dept. of the Interior because of the allegedly obscene nature of his poetry—but which is now considered an inescapable part of the rise of American culture in the 19th century.

■ Interested crowds getting their first glimpse of a new wonder of the world, the arm and torch of **The Statue of Liberty** *(left)*, completed by French sculptor Frederic Auguste Bartholdi in time to be exhibited, as illustrated here, at the 1876 Philadelphia Centennial Exhibition. The exhibition was a huge celebration, held in Philadelphia's Fairmount Park, to mark the nation's 100th birthday. It included exhibits of all kinds, especially those marking progress in science and technology. It would be another ten years before the Statue of Liberty was completed and, the problems of financing and construction solved, installed on Bedloe's Island (now called Liberty Island) in New York's harbor. The display of the arm and torch at Philadelphia aroused great interest in the statue, and certainly aided the fundraising drive a few years later which raised the $270,000 needed to erect the pedestal. The French people had contributed an almost equivalent amount for the statue itself.

> *"Genius is one per cent inspiration and ninety-nine per cent perspiration."*
>
> —THOMAS EDISON

■ **The Corliss Engine** *(left)*, one of the scientific marvels exhibited at Philadelphia in 1876. Designed by George S. Corliss of Providence, Rhode Island, it was the largest steam engine ever created, with a 56-ton flywheel which measured 30 feet in diameter.

■ **Thomas Edison** *(above)* with the early version of the phonograph he invented in 1877. A stylus attached to a diaphragm recorded a voice by etching groves into a foil-covered cylinder turned by a hand crank. Another stylus was inserted into the grooves and the crank was turned to play back the voice. In the first demonstration of his machine, Edison recorded a verse of *Mary Had A Little Lamb*. Born in Milan, Ohio in 1847, Edison tinkered with mechanical devices as a child, and later worked as a telegrapher. He improved the telegraphic stock ticker in use on Wall Street, and with the proceeds of his success with that device set up his research laboratory in 1876. In 1877, having already added an improved telephone to his list of successes, he invented the phonograph, which he continued to perfect and develop in the following years. In 1879, Edison was able to demonstrate his revolutionary incandescent light bulb. In all he held over 1,000 patents, making him surely the giant of this great age in American invention and technology. He died in 1931.

■ A Currier and Ives print of a post-Civil War **Mississippi steamboat, The Princess** *(above)* unloading logs along the riverbank. John Fitch demonstrated the first steam-powered boat in America on the Delaware River in 1787, when he carried delegates to the Constitutional Convention in Philadelphia at the speed of three miles per hour. The first steamboat with side paddle wheels was introduced a decade later, and on September 4, 1807 Robert Fulton's *Clermont,* with an improved paddle wheel design, made its first commerical trip up the Hudson between New York and Albany. The first steamboat on the Mississippi, *The New Orleans,* also designed by Fulton, made its maiden voyage on the river in 1812. The Mississippi proved to be the steamboat's natural habitat. In an 1870 contest between two famous Mississippi steamboats, *The Robert E. Lee* and the *Natchez, The Robert E. Lee* won an 1,100 mile race from New Orleans to St. Louis, completing the trip in three days, 18 hours and 14 minutes—more than six hours faster than its rival—as crowds lined the riverbanks all the way to cheer them on. A Mississippi side-wheeler was also involved in the worst marine disaster in the history of the United States. On April 27, 1865, the steamboat *Sultana* was carrying, far in excess of her normal capacity, 2,400 Union soldiers who had just been released from Confederate prison camps, along with at least 100 civilian passengers. Her boiler exploded eight miles from Memphis, Tennessee, and the *Sultana* burned down to the water line. Many passengers were trapped inside, while several hundred survived by clinging to floating debris in the river. At least 1,547 were killed in the *Sultana* disaster, exceeding the 1,513 who were lost when the *Titanic* sank in 1912.

"The youth of America is their oldest tradition. It has been going on now for three hundred years."

—OSCAR WILDE

■ *The Cowboys* by Frederic Remington *(below).* The classical era of the cowboy was a brief one, extending from roughly the end of the Civil War—many cowboys were Civil War veterans—until the mid-1880s. It was during those two decades that cowboy legends were made on the great cattle drives up the Chisholm Trail from Texas to the railheads at the wild western towns in Kansas, and on other long routes to and from the northern Plains. With the advance of barbed wire in the 1880s, the development of the railroad industry, and the taking over of the cattle industry by big business, the era of "the long drives" faded from the western scene.

■ **Shooting Buffalo on the Kansas-Pacific Railroad** *(right, top),* a wood engraving from the early 1870s. During the Civil War there may have been ten to fifteen million buffalo on the Great Plains, perhaps more; by the early 1890s there were only a few hundred. The buffalo was a victim of many groups—Indian fighters who knew that if you kill the buffalo, you kill the Indian; the railroads who employed professional hunters to kill herds of buffalo to feed their workers during the era of railroad construction; sportsmen, as seen in this illustration, who killed them for the fun of it; and, later in the century, suppliers of buffalo leather, which suddenly became fashionable. Only the dedicated work of conservationists saved the buffalo from extinction in the 20th century.

■ **Sitting Bull and Buffalo Bill Cody** *(right, bottom),* photographed in Montreal after 1885. Sitting Bull, leader of the Sioux and victor over Custer in 1876, had been forced in 1883 by famine, after vainly trying to find a permanent home for his people in Canada, to give in to the Federal Government's wish that he live on the reservation. From 1883 he lived at the Standing Rock Agency in South Dakota. For a period after 1885, the Indian agent at Standing Rock, largely to remove Sitting Bull from the scene because he had opposed the sale of tribal lands, allowed him to join Buffalo Bill's Wild West Show. His appearances with the western showman— Sitting Bull was then about 55 years old—made him famous throughout the world. Only a few years later Sitting Bull was caught up in the events leading to the Wounded Knee massacre where he was killed on December 15, 1890.

■ **Workmen on the Brooklyn
Bridge** *(top),* cutting and tying tension
cables as the bridge was nearing completion. Construction began early in
1870. By 1877 the distinctive towers
had been completed and there was a
temporary footpath strung between
them over which a few thousand adventurous New Yorkers walked during the
remaining six years before the bridge
was finished. Eventually the four giant
cables, each of which was made up of
thousands of individual wires like the
ones being tied in this photograph, were
ready to hold the wide roadway of the
completed bridge. When the bridge was
opened there were five roads across it
side by side—two for horse-drawn vehi-
cles, two for trains, and one for pedes-
trians. The cost had been high. Twenty
workmen were killed before the bridge
was finished. The bridge's designer,
John A. Roebling, had been killed in an
accident on a Brooklyn ferry wharf in
1872. His son, Washington Roebling,
the bridge's chief engineer, permanently
disabled by a case of the bends as he
worked in one of the caissons below the
surface of the East River on the bridge's
foundations, spent the last ten years before the bridge was finished in 1883 su-
pervising construction by watching
every activity through a telescope from
his Brooklyn apartment. When completed, the Brooklyn Bridge, known at
the time as the East River Bridge, was
the longest suspension bridge in the
world—its total length was 5,989 feet
with 1,595.5 feet over the river.

■ **The Brooklyn Bridge** *(bottom),*
open for traffic, a wood engraving from
Harper's Weekly for May 26, 1883. At
the opening ceremonies on May 24,
President Chester Alan Arthur walked
across the bridge with a party of digni-
taries; on the following day over
150,000 people followed. New Yorkers
were justifiably proud of this engineering miracle which they had watched take
shape for so long. *Harper's* author Montgomery Schuyler summed it up this
way: "It so happens that the work which
is likely to be our most durable monu-
ment, and which is likely to convey
some knowledge of us to the most re-
mote posterity, is a work of bare utility;
not a shrine, not a fortress, not a pal-
ace, but a bridge."

■ **A baseball game in 1887** *(top),* a lithograph by Prang. The American game of baseball evolved slowly from other games over a long period. It is generally agreed that the first recorded game which approximated baseball as we know it was played on June 19, 1846 at the Elysian Fields in Hoboken, New Jersey between the Knickerbockers and the New York Nine, and was won by the Nine, 23 to one. A New York banker and organizer of the Knickerbocker team, Alexander J. Cartwright, was responsible for the design of the diamond-shaped playing field and for some of the basic rules which are still used, such as nine men on a side and bases 90 feet apart. It differed from the modern game in that pitching was underhand from a mound 45 feet from home plate, and pitchers tried to let batters hit the ball.

"It is by the goodness of God that in our country we have those three unspeakably precious things: freedom of speech, freedom of conscience, and the prudence never to practice either of them."

—MARK TWAIN

■ **Mark Twain** *(bottom),* shortly before his death in 1910 at the age of 74. Born Samuel Clemens in Hannibal, Missouri in 1835, Twain took his *nom de plume* from an expression used by riverboat pilots—one of his early occupations—for gauging the depth of the water. He went west as a newspaperman after the Civil War and in his early stories and sketches, such as *The Celebrated Jumping Frog of Calaveras County* (1865), portrayed California just after the Gold Rush. He gained national recognition with *The Innocents Abroad* in 1869. With the books that followed, Twain established himself as the great American humorist and storyteller, especially through the books which evoke the place and the period in which he grew up— *Life On the Mississippi* (1883) and his two masterpieces, *Tom Sawyer* (1876) and its sequel, *Huckleberry Finn* (1884). Other books such as *The Gilded Age* took a caustic look through the novelist's eye at the materialism of post-Civil War America and *Roughing It* vividly recreated the early days of mining in Nevada in the 1860s. When he died in 1910 Twain was an American institution.

■ **Annie Oakley** *(left),* photographed in the 1880s when she was a star of Buffalo Bill's Wild West Show. Born Phoebe Anne Mozee in Darke County, Ohio in 1860, "Little Sure Shot" as she was known—she was under five feet tall—came to astonish the world with her feats of marksmanship. She could easily shoot a cigarette from between a man's lips, and even a playing card sideways. She once fired at 5,000 targets in a nine-hour period and hit 4,772 of them. She traveled the world with Buffalo Bill, and once shook the hand of Queen Victoria who was suitably impressed with her performance. Annie Oakley was still astonishing audiences in the 1920s when she was over 60. Her legend inspired Irving Berlin's memorable 1946 musical *Annie Get Your Gun.*

■ Apache leader **Geronimo** *(right),* fourth from the left in the front row, with other Apache prisoners outside a railroad car in Arizona in 1886. At the time this photograph was taken Geronimo was almost 60 years old and had been fighting against the incursion, first of Mexico and later of the United States, on his people's native lands in Arizona for over forty years. Geronimo was embittered by the death of his wife and children in a conflict with the Mexicans in 1858. In 1874, 4,000 Apaches were forced by the United States to go to a barren reservation at San Carlos in central Arizona. Geronimo and other Apache leaders led them on a campaign of revenge. In the later 1870s, through the efforts of Lt. Col. George F. Crook, relative peace was restored but could not be maintained by Crook's successors; at that time Geronimo and his followers once again left the reservation. In 1882 Crook returned to Arizona to deal with Geronimo and forced him to surrender in 1884. The following year, however, Geronimo and a small band fled the San Carlos reservation again. After a ten-month campaign, Geronimo again surrendered to Crook on March 27, 1886, but soon thereafter escaped again. Crook was replaced by Brigadier General Nelson A. Miles. For five months, 5,000 of Miles's troops hunted Geronimo and his small band, and finally induced the Apache leader to surrender again in September, 1886. For the rest of his life Geronimo was a prisoner, first in Florida, and after 1894 in Oklahoma. He never saw Arizona again, and died in 1909.

■ *Police Station Lodgers* (top), photographed at New York's Elizabeth Street station by Jacob Riis in 1890, the year Riis published his shocking documentary on conditions in New York's tenements, *How the Other Half Lives.* Born in Denmark in 1849, Riis emigrated to America in 1870 and within a few years became a police reporter on New York's Lower East Side. He was appalled at conditions—such as an infant mortality rate as high as one in ten—in the area's tenements which housed mostly immigrants, and he began to document his observations with photographs. *How the Other Half Lives,* illustrated in its first edition mostly with line drawings based on Riis's photographs, helped bring about the first legislation to curb the worst evils of the tenement houses. Though conditions for the average immigrant did not improve dramatically overnight, Riis's work had an impact in his day, and foreshadowed that of the great muckraking journalists of the first decades of the 20th century.

■ A graphic illustration of the incredible devastation caused by the **Johnstown Flood** *(bottom).* On May 31, 1889, after two days of heavy rain, the earth dam of the South Fork Reservoir, in the hills above the town of Johnstown in south-central Pennsylvania, gave way, sending a tidal wave of water onto the town below. Unable to avoid the flood in the less than 45 minutes it took the reservoir to empty, more than 2,200 people were killed, and virtually every building in the path of the descending wave was swept away. Johnstown was literally obliterated in the worst flood in American history.

■ **Pittsburgh in the 1890s** *(opposite),* a city which developed around the Carnegie steel mills, part of the new urban-industrial landscape at the end of the 19th century. This was a time of confident empire-building in the industrial world. Such concerns as the consumption of energy, the dissipation of natural resources, and, above all, the pollution of the atmosphere and the devastation of the planet's ecology were not yet public issues.

55

The Oklahoma Land Rush *(above),* a photograph taken shortly after the noon starting guns on April 22, 1889 opened two million acres in present-day Oklahoma, which had been set aside as Indian Territory in 1834, to settlement by homesteaders. Would-be settlers rushed across the borders of the former Indian Territory—which had also served for years as a place of refuge for those on the run from the law in neighboring states and territories—on horseback, bicycles, carriages, wagons, and on foot. They came across the southern border of Kansas, the western border of Arkansas, and the northern border of Texas; within nine hours after the guns sounded, all two million acres had been claimed by land-hungry homesteaders who numbered at least 50,000. This 1889 land rush added a word to the language of the region; a certain number tried to get across the starting lines before the noon guns. These settlers, who tried to get there "sooner"—many were turned back—gave Oklahoma, which became a state in 1907, its nickname.

Frederick Douglass *(right),* escaped slave, orator, leader of the Abolitionist movement, and author of one of the basic books on the struggle of blacks for freedom and equality in the United States, *The Life and Times of Frederick Douglass,* first published in 1845, revised and completed in 1882. Born into slavery in Maryland in 1817, Douglass was taught to read by a woman to whose house he had been sent by his owner to work as a servant. After having been forced to return to work as a field hand, Douglass eventually escaped in 1838, first to New York City and then to New Bedford, Massachusetts. During this period he changed his name to Douglass—he had been born Frederick Augustus Washington Bailey—to escape slave hunters. Asked to describe his experiences, Douglass discovered his literary and oratorical gifts and began to work with the Massachusetts Anti-Slavery Society. In the 1840s he wrote the first version of his autobiography and went on a lengthy speaking tour of Great Britain and Ireland. Back in the United States, Douglass was able to purchase his freedom and to start his own newspaper, which he published in support of the Abolitionist cause from 1847 to 1860. During the Civil War, Douglass urged Lincoln, who valued his advice, to press for the abolition of slavery, and to arm former slaves to fight for the North. In the period of Reconstruction he pressed the struggle for civil rights for blacks and women, and in his later years, as U.S. Minister and consul general to Haiti, and in other posts, Douglass was the first black to hold high office in the government of the United States.

"The destiny of the colored American . . . is the destiny of America."

—FREDERICK DOUGLASS

■ **Striking steel workers** *(below),* on a hillside overlooking the Carnegie Steel Company's mills at Homestead, Pennsylvania during the Homestead Strike of 1892. The strike had begun in July when Carnegie Steel demanded a salary cut from 800 skilled members of the Amalgamated Association of Iron and Steel Workers. Three thousand unskilled workers joined the Amalgamated members in a well-organized strike. When Carnegie tried to bring in 300 Pinkerton Detective Agency operatives to take control of the plant on July 6, they found themselves in a pitched battle with the strikers. The Pinkertons were forced to retreat after seven of their men were killed and 13 wounded; six days later the state militia opened the plant to strikebreakers. The striking steel workers held out for five months and then capitulated; the brutal strike and its aftermath delayed the full unionization of the steel industry for decades.

■ Financier **J. P. Morgan** *(below),* a photographic portrait by Edward Steichen. Morgan became a dominant figure on the American financial scene by reorganizing several major railroads between 1885 and 1900. Just after the turn of the century, he created the largest company in the world at that time when he bought Andrew Carnegie's steel enterprises for $250 million and combined them with other firms to form U.S. Steel. He played his greatest public role, however, at the age of 71 in 1907, during a financial panic triggered by a run on the Knickerbocker Trust Company and the Trust Company of America. With other banks vulnerable, Morgan assembled the nation's leading financiers in his New York offices and forced them to join him in pledging $25 million to save the banking system. President Theodore Roosevelt had no option but to suspend, for a while at least, his attacks on the "malefactors of great wealth" he was fond of castigating, and to endorse Morgan's plan.

■ **"The Breakers"** *(left),* Cornelius Vanderbilt's Newport, Rhode Island mansion, built at a cost of $5,000,000, a symbol of the wealth of the 1890s. Founded in 1639 by a group of dissident Puritans from Massachusetts, Newport flourished as a port in colonial times. With its great climate and easy train and boat connections to New York and other eastern cities, Newport developed after the Civil War as an opulent summer resort where families from the social and financial elite of American society outdid each other in building suitable "cottages" for the summer months.

■ **The bodies of Indians massacred at Wounded Knee Creek** *(top)* on South Dakota's Pine Ridge Reservation on December 29, 1890. The causes of the Wounded Knee massacre were many. Threatened by hunger and disease during a bad winter, the Sioux at Wounded Knee became deeply involved in the relatively new Ghost Dance Religion, a cult which promised the resurrection of dead ancestors and buffalo and the coming of an Indian Messiah who would sweep away the White Man. As a precaution, the authorities decided to arrest the legendary Sioux chief Sitting Bull, a believer in the Ghost Dance, who had lived on the reservation off and on for several years. Sitting Bull was seized on December 15; a battle erupted between the police who had taken him and Sitting Bull's supporters in which Sitting Bull and several policemen were killed. Fearing reprisals, another Sioux chief, Big Foot, led a band of 350 of his people to one of their old camps on the Cheyenne River. Intercepted by the cavalry, the Indians were taken instead to a camp on Wounded Knee Creek. When a troop of about 500 soldiers demanded their weapons, the final battle broke out. The Indians were no match for a larger force of cavalry supported by cannons. About 25 soldiers and 153 Indians, including Big Foot, were killed—half of the Sioux killed were women and children. The Indian Wars were finally over.

■ **The Ferris Wheel at the 1892 World Columbian Exposition** *(middle)* on Chicago's South Side, a huge celebration of the 400th anniversary of Columbus's discovery of America. In the fabulous "White City" of classicly designed buildings, exhibits were held displaying evidence of the progress of mankind. The Ferris Wheel was one of the Exposition's most popular novelties—the exotic dancer "Little Egypt," and the replicas of Columbus's three ships were others. Designed by George W.G. Ferris, the giant wheel, 250 feet in diameter, held 36 boxes, each big enough for several people to stand in while they were carried up and around the wheel. The Exposition was a huge success; unfortunately most of the buildings burned down on January 8, 1894, just a few months after the Exposition closed.

■ Composer and bandleader **John Philip Sousa** *(bottom)* posing in 1917 with the 12th Coast Artillery Band. Sousa led the famed Marine Corps Band from 1880 to 1892; during those years his name became synonymous with military music. After 1892, Sousa led his own band on tours across the United States and around the world. The 140 marches he composed include some of the most popular ever written—"The Stars and Stripes Forever" (1896), "Semper Fidelis" (1888), and "The Washington Post" (1889).

■ Founder of a great American industrial empire, **Henry Ford** *(left),* in 1896 with his first "horseless carriage." Ford was only one of a number of inventors tinkering with the idea of the automobile in the last two decades of the 19th century. Who came first in this area has never been definitively established. The first American automobile patent was applied for by George B. Selden in 1879, but he had not at that time built a car. Selden managed to keep the patent pending for 16 years, and finally received it in 1895. It is known, however, that Charles E. and J. Frank Duryea designed and built a gasoline-powered one-cylinder automobile, which first ran on September 21, 1893. Meanwhile, some automotive historians back the claims of John William Lambert of Ohio City, Ohio for an internal combustion automobile which he designed in 1890 and ran in 1891. Many other inventors and engineers were actively working on primitive automobiles during those same years. Whoever came first, there is little question about who became most successful; within twenty years from the time depicted in this picture, Ford's assembly lines would be turning out the Model T by the tens of thousands.

■ Prospectors in the **Alaska Gold Rush of 1898** *(above)* checking the main street of a mining town for gold deposits. When the first census that included Alaska was taken in 1880, it was found that the whole territory had only 33,000 inhabitants, of whom all but 430 were natives. The 1898 Gold Rush, the last such major gold rush in the present-day 50 states, brought an immediate influx of 30,000 eager prospectors to Alaska, giving the settlement of the territory a boost which lasted beyond the time when the rumors of gold strikes were largely played out.

■ **The Battleship _Maine_** _(opposite, top)_, after having been blown up and sunk in Havana harbor on February 15, 1898, the prelude to the Spanish-American War. Despite the climate of agitation against Spain on the part of America's "yellow press" led by William Randolph Hearst, Joseph Pulitzer and others who supported the idea of Cuban independence, and who seemed to want a war with Spain for any reason they could find, President McKinley had sent the _Maine_ to Havana as a gesture of friendship with the Spanish. The gesture backfired; responsibility for the sinking was never fixed, but the American press and popular opinion blamed the Spanish. Two hundred and sixty American sailors were killed when the _Maine_ sank.

■ **Col. Theodore Roosevelt and the "Rough Riders"** _(opposite, bottom),_ the First Volunteer Cavalry, which Roosevelt commanded in Cuba. The Spanish-American War was inevitable after the _Maine._ Urged on by the tremendous press campaign, Congress declared Cuba independent on April 19, 1898. On April 24, Spain declared war on America, and the following day America followed suit. While Roosevelt and his cavalry were getting ready for action in Cuba, Commodore George Dewey sailed into Manila harbor in the Philippines and took the city from Spain on May 1.

■ **The United States Army charging up San Juan Hill** _(above)_ in the decisive land action of the war in Cuba. On July 1, the 10,000-man American force under General William Shafter, including Roosevelt and his Rough Riders, attacked the crucial Spanish position on San Juan Hill outside the city of Santiago de Cuba, on Cuba's southeastern coast. The Spanish forces were outnumbered but well dug in; the United States forces took the hill, but suffered a thousand casualties. The Spanish position was rendered untenable when the American navy destroyed their fleet off Santiago de Cuba on July 3. On July 17, the Spanish command surrendered; it was recorded that General Shafter was delighted at the prospect of getting his men off the island before the wet season brought malaria. By the treaty ending the war, Cuba gained her independence, though the island was placed under American military control for three years. The United States acquired Guam, Puerto Rico, and the Philippines. Spain received $20,000,000 from the United States.

"A man who is good enough to shed his blood for his country is good enough to be given a square deal afterwards."

—THEODORE ROOSEVELT

■ **Susan B. Anthony** *(left)*, photographed at her desk in 1898 during the period, 1892–1900, when she was president of the National American Woman Suffrage Association. Born in 1820 in Adams, Massachusetts, Anthony acquired an interest in the Abolitionist movement from her Quaker father. She campaigned vigorously for various anti-slavery societies in the years leading up to the Civil War. After the war, while publishing the liberal weekly *The Revolution* in association with Elizabeth Cady Stanton in New York, Anthony argued that women should be entitled to the same rights which blacks had acquired under the Fourteenth and Fifteenth Amendments. For the rest of her life she worked for the cause of women's suffrage, both in the United States and with various international organizations. She died in 1906 at the age of 86, fourteen years before women in America gained the right to vote.

■ A slice of backwoods Americana, **the Hatfield family** *(right),* photographed by T. F. Hunt in 1899 during the progress of their legendary feud with the McCoys. The feud started in the 1880s with accusations against the West Virginia Hatfields of stealing a hog and murdering three McCoys from neighboring Kentucky. Eventually the McCoys staged a raid on the Hatfields's home, took nine prisoners and brought them in for trial. This unusual initiative was upheld by the courts and the Hatfields were convicted.

"Here, in the first paragraph of the Declaration [of Independence], is the assertion of the natural right of all to the ballot; for how can 'the consent of the governed' be given, if the right to vote be denied?"

—SUSAN B. ANTHONY

The American Century

LOOKING BACK AT EARLIER EPOCHS of American history, it seems from our perspective on the brink of the 21st century that individual eras in American history once lasted a much longer time—the Colonial period from 1607 to 1775, the Antebellum South from the first plantations in the seventeenth century to 1861. In the 20th century, history has speeded up; generations come and go faster—we can look back over less then a hundred years and discern a multitude of individual eras, each with its own special quality.

The Spanish-American War and the building of the Panama Canal thrust a confident America onto the world scene to assume the position to which vast industrial and economic growth in the last decades of the 19th century seemed to many to entitle us. The Progressive Era in domestic politics attempted to deal with some of the new problems of this modern world in which we found ourselves after the turn of the century, problems of industrial regulation, unplanned urban growth, corrupt machine politics. By tipping the scales in Europe in World War I, America consolidated her position as a world power; by rejecting President Wilson's League of Nations once the war was over, we sank back toward isolationism again, seeming to recoil from foreign involvement as quickly as we had accepted it. The Jazz Age of the 1920s was a time of relaxation and easy entertainment; the Depression of the 1930s a period of foundering despair enlivened by Roosevelt's New Deal, a new expanded role for the federal government in the life of the Republic. World War II made us fight against great powers on both sides of the globe at once. We won both "the good war" against Nazi ideology and confirmation of our place in the family of nations; we witnessed the start of the nuclear age. In the late 1940s we expected another period of consolidation, but had hardly become accustomed to peace before Korea brought us back onto the world scene. The 1950s were the fight against communism, real and imagined, and the flight to the suburbs; the 1960s were about Vietnam, protest, racial conflict, rock music, and space exploration. Watergate colored the 1970s, Reagan and the new Conservatism the 1980s; the 1990s began with an echo of Cuba, Korea, and Vietnam in the deserts of the Middle East and the astonishing end of the American-Soviet Cold War.

It is easy to forget that there are always other sides to our historical coins. Our adventure in Cuba brought forth a howl of protest here at home, now largely forgotten. There were many Americans who regretted the failure of Wilson's League, many more who never drank illegal liquor in the roaring twenties. There were businesses which prospered in the Depression, Republicans who applauded the New Deal, Senators in the 1950s who didn't think there was a communist lurking in every shadow. We had social critics who found the suburbs stultifying before the first wave of crabgrass had emerged, others who thought our voyage to the moon a waste of time. In the complicated record of this rich, fascinating, and contradictory century, the historian can find something for everyone.

In the long history of human miscalculation, the one which the leaders of Germany made in January, 1917 to engage in total submarine warfare against all shipping, neutral as well as belligerent, has never received the attention it deserves. Germany's submarine campaign had already given the United States enough provocation to enter a dozen wars, but Wilson, reflecting the essential isolationism of his period, had engaged instead in a long, elaborate ritual of meeting atrocities with diplomatic protests which, if they didn't stop the killing, probably slowed it down, and he had kept the United States out of the war, which is what a majority of his constituents seemed to want. Germany knew that the new submarine campaign would bring the United States in; her leaders calculated that Britain would be starved into submission before the United States could mobilize enough men and equipment to make a difference. They were wrong. From a standing start, the United States raised an army of four million men under the Selective Service Act of 1917; 1,200,000 of these American soldiers were in France with General Pershing by September, 1918. Two months later, the war was over; Germany was forced to accept onerous peace terms, which among other consequences, helped make her vulnerable within a decade and a half to Hitler's spellbinding rhetoric.

If we look at the history of this century to find one small period which made the greatest difference, which saw the most fundamental change in the nature of American life, we could hardly do better than to take up the famous first 100 days of the New Deal, the start of the first Administration of Franklin Delano Roosevelt, who took office on March 4, 1933 declaring in the midst of a crisis in economic confidence that "the only thing we have to fear is fear itself." In order to restore some measure of hope and stability, Roosevelt sent to Congress, between March 4 and mid-June, 1933, recommendations and legislation dealing with the banking crisis, unemployment relief, agricultural recovery, the securities industry, railroad and industrial recovery, the Tennessee Valley Authority, and home foreclosures. Congress enacted every measure requested by the Administration. While many of Roosevelt's programs were failures, and the economic recovery he sought was long in coming, the precedent had been established for massive governmental intrusion into virtually every area of the nation's life in a way that would have been unheard of a few short decades earlier. The break with the politics of the Republic's first century and a half was clear-cut; events have showed that, despite the sometimes hopeful rhetoric of those who claim to long for a simpler age, there simply is no going back.

As they have been in every century, the daily lives of average Americans were transformed over and over again in this one. The flood of immigration stopped, not from natural causes, but by law. Under pressure from organized labor, low quotas were set soon after the turn of the century—a total of only 164,000 immigrants were allowed into the United States in 1924, very different from the tidal waves at the end of the nineteenth century. Automobiles very quickly were everywhere; air travel became commonplace. Spectator sports evolved into a complex of huge industries. Movies became the nation's popular entertainment. At the turn of the century, the film industry barely existed; in the 1920s, 50 million people a week went to the movies and clamored for more. Radio brought entertainment into every home; television so captured the nation's interest after World War II that there were fears for the future of the film industry. While film found a way to survive and prosper in the television age, the transistor and the computer revolutionized every sort of mundane activity. Americans became used to change at a pace their ancestors would not have been able to grasp.

The United States was no better prepared for the start of World War II, but we had learned in World War I that one thing Americans are good at is the quick mobilization of resources. Nothing could have prepared the country for the scale of the second world conflict. Fifteen million men and women went into uniform; millions more took war-related jobs. By 1944, American industry was producing more than twice as much military material as our enemies combined; by the end of the war, we had turned out 6,500 ships, 296,400 airplanes and 86,330 tanks. We had also, at a cost of two billion dollars, created a workable atomic bomb, first tested in July, 1945, and used a month later to end the war with Japan. Americans would spend many years contemplating the fact that they were the first inhabitants of the earth possessing the power to destroy it. The development of nuclear weapons gave the international politics of the Cold War years a quality which they had never had before. The centuries-long period when international power was divided among several nations of roughly equal and continually shifting strength was over. Now there were only two super powers, and the political center of the world was gone from Europe. In Korea, in Southeast Asia, in the Middle East the nation learned something over the last few decades about the limitations which great power brings in its wake in a nuclear age; if there is a hopeful note at the end of the first 500 years, it was struck most loudly by the falling of the Berlin Wall.

■ **An Immigrant from Southern Europe** *(opposite, top left)* leaving the Ellis Island Ferry holding her papers, photographed c. 1900. Ellis Island in upper New York Bay was the federal government's main immigration station from 1892 until 1943. During that period millions of immigrants from all parts of the world passed through the Ellis Island facility. The major new trend at the turn of the century was the increase in the percentage of immigrants coming from southern Europe, particularly from Italy, and from Russia, as Jews fled the religious persecution which was widespread under the Czarist regime.

■ **Immigrant children** *(opposite, top right)* being examined by a New York City health inspector after arriving at the Battery from Ellis Island during a typhus scare in 1911.

■ Immigrants having **lunch at Ellis Island** in 1920 *(opposite, bottom left)*.

■ **An Italian mother with her three children** *(opposite, bottom right)*, photographed by Lewis Hine at Ellis Island, 1905.

■ **Immigrants on the deck of the steamship *Kroonland*** *(above)*, arriving at Ellis Island in September, 1920.

'Give me your tired, your poor,
Your huddled masses yearning to breathe free,
The wretched refuse of your teeming shore,
Send these, the homeless, tempest-tossed, to me:
I lift my lamp beside the golden door.'

—EMMA LAZARUS

[INSCRIPTION FOR THE STATUE OF LIBERTY]

■ **Orville and Wilbur Wright** (*opposite, top left*) of Dayton, Ohio, inventors of the airplane, with which in 1903 they achieved the first powered, sustained flight of a heavier-than-air craft. The Wright brothers developed their mechanical and aeronautical skills working with bicycles, kites and gliders before trying their first airplane. **An epoch-making photograph** (*opposite, top right*), taken at Kill Devil Hill near Kitty Hawk, North Carolina on December 17, 1903, shows Orville Wright at the controls between the wings of their 605-pound biplane, *the Flyer*, with Wilbur running alongside. Their homemade 13-horsepower engine had just powered the two-propellor plane, which cost about $1,000 to build, into the air for its first flight; it covered 120 feet and lasted 12 seconds. They flew four times that day—on the last flight Wilbur stayed aloft for 59 seconds and a distance of 852 feet.

■ **Helen Keller** (*opposite, bottom left*) at 23 as she graduated *cum laude* from Radcliffe College in 1904. Deaf and blind due to illness from the age of 19 months, Keller, who shortly thereafter became mute as well, began in 1887 to work with the teacher who would change her life, Anne Mansfield Sullivan. Within two years Keller was able to read and write in Braille. At Radcliffe, Sullivan translated Keller's lectures for her, "spelling" them into her hand so she could understand them. Keller devoted her life to helping the deaf and blind, touring the world to promote education for those with disabilities similar to hers, and writing many books including *The Story of My Life* (1902) and *Helen Keller's Journal* (1938).

■ *The Great Train Robbery* (*opposite, bottom right*). 1894 saw the opening of 'Kinetoscope' parlors in major cities around the United States. The Kinetoscope, invented by Thomas Edison, was a 'peep-show' device in which one person at a time could view a brief motion picture. These first pictures showed such scenes as a blacksmith at an anvil, a boxing match, and in one case an Edison employee with a prodigious mustache emitting a monumental sneeze. Within a few years, projection devices had been created to allow the showing of films to audiences in theaters. As the technical ability to show films developed, so did the films themselves. An Edison director, Edwin W. Porter, is credited with being the first to exploit the idea of narrative continuity. In 1903 Porter directed a film which showed firefighters rushing to save a mother and child in a burning house. That same year Porter created a film landmark in *The Great Train Robbery*, from which a still is shown here. Shot in New Jersey and running an unprecedented almost 12 minutes, *The Great Train Robbery* was a continuous, logical narrative with a beginning, a middle and an end. Crowds jammed theaters to see this new feature.

■ **The San Francisco Earthquake** (*above*). Troops on the watch for looters patrolling San Francisco's Market Street in the aftermath of the fire and earthquake which struck in the early morning of April 18, 1906. Over four square miles of the city were turned to ruins and more than 28,000 buildings of all descriptions were destroyed—some were blown up with dynamite in attempts to stop the advancing flames with backfires. This was not the first earthquake to rock San Francisco—others had occurred in 1868, 1898 and 1900—but it was the most destructive. Approximately 1,000 people were killed and a quarter of a million were left homeless. It was estimated at the time that insurance claims were paid totaling over $300,000,000, although many firms were unable to meet their obligations.

■ Magician **Harry Houdini** *(top)*, seated with his shoes off, holding a bell between his feet to expose one of the techniques used by fraudulent mediums, spiritualists and other charlatans. Born Erik Weisz in Budapest in 1874, the son of a rabbi, Houdini took his stage name from an 18th century French conjuror, Jean-Eugène Robert-Houdin. As a performer, Houdini's speciality was extricating himself from confined positions in which he was often first shackled and then locked, either underwater in a weighted trunk or suspended in air wearing a straitjacket. Houdini wrote several classic books on magic, including *The Unmasking of Robert-Houdin* (1908), *Miracle Mongers and Their Methods* (1920), and *A Magician Among the Spirits* (1924).

■ **Theodore Roosevelt and naturalist John Muir** *(middle)* at Glacier Point above Yosemite Valley, California. Few individuals ever left their mark on an era so completely as Roosevelt, who became President when McKinley was assassinated in 1901, and was elected in his own right in 1904. His tenure was marked by his opposition to big business and to monopolies of vital industries. He was responsible for the federal government's antitrust actions against several industrial giants, including Standard Oil of New Jersey. Explorer, soldier, prolific author, leader of the "Rough Riders" in the Spanish-American War, Roosevelt set aside large amounts of federal land for conservation—one of his most important legacies. Muir, born in Scotland in 1838, emigrated with his family to Wisconsin in 1849. By the end of the 1860s he had decided to devote his life to the study of nature, and he explored the wilderness regions of the Far West over and over again. An early advocate of forest conservation, Muir campaigned for the establishment of the Sequoia and Yosemite national parks, which came about in 1890, and he continued thereafter to press for conservation. He was a natural ally of Roosevelt's; this photograph was taken during a 1903 camping trip they made together in the Yosemite region.

■ Physicist **Albert A. Michelson** *(bottom)* in his laboratory at the University of Chicago, where he was Chairman of the Physics Department after 1892. In 1887, with his colleague Edward W. Morley, Michelson discovered that light has a constant speed in a vacuum; he also measured the speed of light with a high degree of accuracy. Michelson and Morley's work led to the 1905 proposal by Einstein that the speed of light is a universal constant. Michelson was awarded the Nobel Prize for Physics in 1907; he was the first American scientist to be so honored.

"Most people are on *the world, not in it—having no conscious sympathy of relationship to anything about them—undiffused, separate, and rigidly alone like marbles of polished stone, touching but separate."*

—JOHN MUIR

■ Heavyweight champion **Jack Johnson** *(opposite, top)* at Reno, Nevada on July 4, 1910, having just knocked out James J. Jeffries, the former champion and "white hope" who had come out of retirement to try to regain his title. Johnson had become the first black to win the title when he knocked out Tommy Burns in Sydney, Australia on December 26, 1908. A target of white supremacists, largely because he was twice married to white women, Johnson was convicted in 1912 of having violated the Mann Act by transporting his wife across state lines before they were married. Released pending appeal of his one-year sentence, Johnson escaped to Canada disguised as a member of a black professional baseball team. He successfully defended his title in Paris three times, but lost in Havana on April 5, 1915 to Jess Willard by knockout in the 26th round. Johnson finally surrendered in 1920, and served his prison sentence; he died in an automobile accident in 1946.

■ **Young coal miners** *(opposite, bottom left)*, photographed by Lewis Hine at South Pittston, Pennsylvania in 1911. The employment of children under 16 for this sort of work, a rampant abuse in the first century of industrialization in America, was first prohibited in the United States only by the Fair Labor Standards Act of 1938, part of Franklin D. Roosevelt's New Deal.

■ **Admiral Robert E. Peary** *(below)* in the cold-weather gear he wore during the decades he spent in polar exploration. On his 1905 attempt to reach the North Pole, Peary penetrated as far north as 87°6′N. latitude from his base at Cape Sheridan, Ellsmere Island, but adverse weather prevented him from reaching his goal. Most scholars believe that Peary finally reached the Pole on April 6, 1909, on his third and final attempt, accompanied at the end by his associate Matthew Henson, a black American, and four Eskimos, but the controversy over who reached the Pole first—Peary or his one-time colleague, Dr. Frederick A. Cook—has never been definitively resolved.

■ **Curtiss Biplane** *(left)*. By 1909 the Wright brothers had a contract with the Army for the world's first military plane, but they also now had competitors. Just a few years after the Wrights' first flight, Glenn Curtiss was upsetting military strategists by 'bombing' ships with oranges dropped from his planes. This led to a Curtiss demonstration of a primitive aircraft carrier. On November 14, 1910, as pictured here, pilot Eugene Ely took off from an 83-foot wooden platform attached to the *U.S.S. Birmingham* and flew this Curtiss X biplane two miles to Hampton Roads, Virginia.

■ A photographer setting up his equipment north of New York's **Flatiron Building** *(opposite, bottom left)* at the intersection of Broadway, Fifth Avenue and 23rd Street, not long after the three-sided, twenty-story structure opened in 1902. Designed for the Fuller Construction Company by Chicago-based architect Daniel H. Burnham, this early and aptly-named skyscraper was briefly the world's tallest. Legend has it that New Yorkers waited for "Burnham's Folly" to be blown down by the first strong wind; almost a century later it still stands, now dwarfed on all sides by the towers of present-day Manhattan.

■ **Jim Thorpe** *(opposite, top right),* one of the greatest and most versatile athletes in the history of American sports, competing in the shot-put in the 1912 Olympic Games at Stockholm. Of Sauk and Fox Indian descent, Thorpe first made his mark on the American sporting scene as an All-American halfback on Coach Glenn "Pop" Warner's Carlisle (Pa.) Indian Industrial School teams. In the 1912 Olympics, Thorpe won gold medals in the decathlon and pentathlon, but was forced to surrender them when it was revealed that he had previously played professional baseball. From 1913 to 1919, Thorpe played the outfield for New York, Cincinnati and Boston in the National League, compiling a .252 batting average in 289 games. Turning to professional football in 1919, Thorpe became one of the pro game's first stars, and was later a charter member of the Professional Football Hall of Fame. In 1982 his Olympic medals were restored to his family.

■ **Knute Rockne** *(opposite, bottom right)* in his 1913 Notre Dame uniform, the year in which the passing of quarterback Gus Dorais to Rockne helped Notre Dame defeat Army and popularized the forward pass, a weapon previously little used in college football. In 1918 the Norwegian-born Rockne became Notre Dame's head coach and his record during the next 13 seasons—105 wins, 12 losses and 5 ties—established Notre Dame at the top of the collegiate football world. Notre Dame was undefeated five times during Rockne's tenure and was recognized as national champion in 1924, 1929 and 1930. The success his teams had on the field and his lively, magnetic personality made Rockne a pivotal figure in American sports during the 1920s. He died in an airplane crash on March 31, 1931.

■ **Ty Cobb** *(top),* sliding into third base. One of the greatest baseball players of all time—Cobb was the leading vote-getter in the Hall of Fame's first election in 1936—and the dominant player in the decade between 1910 and 1920. Cobb played the outfield for Detroit for 22 years, 1905–1926, and finished his career with two seasons with the Philadelphia Athletics. He led the American League in batting 12 times, including nine years in a row, 1907–1915, and compiled the highest-ever lifetime batting average, .367, a record which may never be equaled. Cobb's career hit-total of 4,191 stood as the record until eclipsed by Pete Rose in 1985. Cobb, "The Georgia Peach," was known as a fierce competitor, nowhere more than on the basepaths.

■ An early sign of the transformation that the automobile would bring to America, the first **Standard Oil Filling Station** *(middle),* established in Columbus, Ohio in 1912 in a garage at the corner of Young and Oak Streets.

■ Workers on the **Ford Motor Company** *(bottom)* assembly line at Highland Park, Michigan, dropping the engine into a Model T in 1913. Henry Ford founded the Ford Motor Company in 1903. In 1908 he introduced the Model T, the car that revolutionized the automobile industry. It was a strong but lightweight car, easy to make and easy to repair, with a four-cylinder 20-horsepower engine. It could be produced cheaply and quickly—"in any color so long as it's black," Ford liked to say—on innovative but still primitive assembly lines with a price of about $850. In 1909 Ford sold over 17,000 Model T's, but this was just the beginning. By the time this photograph was taken, the Ford assembly lines had the Model T chassis pulled by a windlass across a 250-foot factory floor as workmen with specialized tasks added parts along the way. The time needed to produce one car had been reduced to six hours from 13 and the price was lowered to $440. In 1913, over 180,000 Model T's were produced, and by 1927, when the Model T was replaced by the Model A, over 15 million had been sold.

■ **Suffragettes** *(above)* on parade in
New York City in 1912. The ratification
of the 19th Amendment in 1920 marked
the success of the women's suffrage
movement in the United States after decades of debates and demonstrations.
America was not the first nation in
which women gained the right to vote—
that honor went to New Zealand in
1893, and Australia, Finland, Norway
and Sweden all saw women voting before the United States. With the vote
came an increased role in politics. Mrs.
Nellie Taylor Ross of Wyoming became
in 1925 the first woman elected governor of a state, and Mrs. Hattie Caraway
of Arkansas became in 1932 the first
woman elected to the United States
Senate.

*"No woman can call herself
free who does not own and
control her body."*

—MARGARET SANGER

■ **Margaret Sanger** *(right)* in 1916, the year in which she opened, in Brooklyn, the first birth control clinic in the United States. As a nurse on New York's Lower East Side just after the turn of the century, Sanger became convinced of the need to disseminate accurate birth control information. A tireless worker on behalf of the birth control movement, Sanger overcame many legal obstacles, including a brief term of imprisonment in 1917, to distribute her publications on contraception. She founded the American Birth Control League in 1921 and was later president of the International Planned Parenthood Federation.

■ The sinking of the ***Titanic*** *(above),* as conceived by German artist Willy Stoewer. On the night of April 14–15, 1912, the new White Star liner *Titanic,* the largest and most luxurious ship in the world, sank less than three hours after striking an iceberg in the North Atlantic, 95 miles south of the Great Banks of Newfoundland. The 46,000-ton *Titanic* was on her maiden voyage, four days out from Southampton, England en route to New York with 2,224 people on board. Of these, 1,513, including many prominent Americans, were drowned and 711 survived in lifeboats until rescued by the Cunard liner *Carpathia,* which arrived on the scene an hour and 20 minutes after the *Titanic* went down. It was later found that another liner, the *Californian,* was less than 20 miles from the *Titanic* when she sank, but had no radio operator on duty to receive the *Titanic's* distress signal.

■ **Jack London** *(right),* one of the most popular American writers, and said to have been, in the years just before World War I, the highest-paid author in America. Born in 1876 in San Francisco, London was largely self-taught; he gained experience which would serve him as a writer during his travels as a sailor, a hobo, and later as a prospector in the Klondike Gold Rush of 1897. A wide reader, he developed a sort of crude socialism as a vital element in many of his novels, though the books for which he is most remembered today deal with the struggle for survival in the wilderness, including those based on his Alaskan adventures, *Call of the Wild* (1903), *White Fang* (1906) and *Burning Daylight* (1910). He died at the age of 40, possibly a suicide, from an overdose of drugs.

■ A walking symbol of the heroic age of American capitalism, **John D. Rockefeller, Sr.** *(below),* seen here at age 76 with his son, John D. Rockefeller, Jr. After he opened his first oil refinery near Cleveland in 1863 with a $4,000 investment, Rockefeller's fortunes grew with the new industry that his Standard Oil Company (Ohio) and its allies soon came to dominate. Despite efforts to break up Standard's monopoly, Rockefeller amassed the fortune which by 1900 had reached perhaps $200,000,000, and had the press describing him as the world's richest man. With his interests transferred to a new holding company, Standard Oil (New Jersey), in a state then more tolerant of monopoly-dominated industries, Rockefeller, Sr. turned his attention after 1897 exclusively to philanthropy. Attacks against the power of Rockefeller's industrial empire were not abated by his generosity. The target in 1904 of one of the classics of muckraking literature, Ida Tarbell's *The History of the Standard Oil Company,* which exposed the ruthless tactics Standard Oil had used to reach and consolidate its position, Rockefeller's corporation was the subject in the following decade of a massive antitrust suit launched by President Theodore Roosevelt. In 1911 the Supreme Court ordered Standard Oil to give up its holdings in 37 related companies. Rockefeller's personal financial position was, however, unassailable; World War I brought with it the inflation that made him the nation's first billionaire by 1916. He died in 1937, two years and two months short of his 100th birthday.

■ Aviators of the World War I **Lafayette Escadrille** *(above),* the volunteer corps of American pilots who fought in the air war for France against Germany during the period before America declared war on the Central Powers, photographed in France on February 16, 1917. Note the lion cub mascot on the lap of the flyer in the front row.

■ A young **Eddie Rickenbacker** *(above),* on the left in this photograph, in the World War I uniform of the 94th Aero Pursuit Squadron. A former racing car driver, Rickenbacker became a fighter pilot in World War I with the help of visionary military aviation enthusiast Col. William (Billy) Mitchell, for whom Rickenbacker first served as a driver. In action, Rickenbacker won 26 air battles and many decorations including the Congressional Medal of Honor. The most celebrated American airman of World War I, Rickenbacker in later years was primarily associated with Eastern Air Lines as a senior executive. In World War II he served on the staff of the Secretary of War; on an inspection trip in 1942 he and several other officers survived being stranded on a raft in the Pacific Ocean for 23 days.

■ The British ocean liner **Lusitania** *(opposite, top),* arriving in New York in September, 1907. Almost eight years later, the sinking of the *Lusitania* by a German U-boat helped precipitate the entry of the United States into World War I. The *Lusitania* was carrying 1,959 passengers en route from New York to Liverpool when it was torpedoed and sunk off the south coast of Ireland on May 7, 1915. The loss of 1,198 passengers, including 128 U.S. citizens, provoked an outcry in the United States in favor of America's immediate declaration of war against Germany. The only action the U.S. Government took, however, was a written protest to the German authorities, who felt justified in sinking the *Lusitania* as the ship was carrying, in addition to its passengers, 173 tons of ammunition for delivery in England. When the United States did finally enter the war in 1917, the German submarine campaign was cited as one of the justifications for that action.

■ Pioneer film director **D.W. Griffith** *(opposite, bottom right),* behind the camera. Griffith is credited with introducing and developing during Hollywood's silent film era many techniques which later became standard, including close-ups, fade-outs, and scenic long shots. In *Birth of A Nation* (1915) and *Intolerance* (1916), Griffith brought silent films to their artistic peak with movies that were longer and more expensively produced than any before. He also contributed to the business side of Hollywood through the success of United Artists, the distributing company he founded in 1919 with Mary Pickford, Charlie Chaplin and Douglas Fairbanks. Griffith made his last film, *The Struggle,* in 1931, though he was then only 56 years old. One of the principal creators of the movie industry, Griffith faded from the Hollywood scene, and died in obscurity in 1948.

■ Cover for the original sheet music for **"Over There"** *(above),* George M. Cohan's classic World War I song, said to have been written on April 6, 1917, the day the United States declared war.

■ **American troops in France in 1918** *(opposite, top).* This photograph, taken at an unidentified location on May 20, 1918, shows American soldiers advancing with the protection of their gas masks. The soldier at left without his mask on, clutches at his throat, overcome by toxic mustard gas. America entered the war against the Central Powers largely in response to Germany's all-out submarine campaign against all shipping, including that of neutral countries. In an historic miscalculation, the Germans felt the submarine campaign would defeat their major opponents and that the United States would not pose much of a threat to them on the battlefield. The United States declared war on Germany on April 6, 1917, almost three years after hostilities had started in Europe. By November, American soldiers were in combat in France.

■ **American troops on the Western Front** *(opposite, bottom),* in an undated photograph, advancing across an overrun German position. The American Expeditionary Force was under the command of General John J. "Black Jack" Pershing. An American colonel, Charles E. Stanton, uttered one of the war's memorable phrases when he said, on arrival with his unit in the summer of 1917, "Lafayette, we are here." American strength in France increased slowly. The first American soldiers to die were killed at Bathélémont, France, on November 2, 1917. The Americans fought their first major battle at Chateau-Thierry in June, 1918.

■ **A French and American raiding party** *(above)* near Badonviller, France in March, 1918. By this time there were 325,000 American soldiers in France. The devastation caused by the years of warfare on an unprecedented scale may be seen in the ruined forests. By November, 1918, though no shots had been fired on German soil, it was clear that the Central Powers could not withstand indefinitely the continually increasing strength of the Allied Armies with an American Expeditionary Force which was approaching a million men. After the Allies scored major victories in the fall of 1918, retaking land that had been lost earlier, the Germans, with no realistic prospects of reversing the tide, requested an armistice. Hostilities ceased on November 11, and the Kaiser abdicated on November 18.

■ The gun which fired the **last shot of World War I** *(below)*—nicknamed "Calamity Jane" and belonging to the 11th Field Artillery— photographed near Meuse, France on the day the fighting stopped, November 11, 1918. The cost of the war was incomprehensible at the time and still staggers the imagination three-quarters of a century later. Perhaps nine million were killed—including 50,585 Americans—in the war that began with the assassination of the Austrian Archduke Ferdinand by a Serbian nationalist in July, 1914.

■ **A wounded black soldier** *(top, left)* watching a parade of the 369th Colored Infantry in New York in 1919, as America's combat troops made their way back from France. American troops were segregated during World War I and continued to be segregated until 1948 when President Truman issued an executive order ending this policy.

■ British Prime Minister David Lloyd George, French President Clemenceau, and President Woodrow Wilson in France at the **Versailles Peace Conference** *(top, right)* in 1919. As Americans paraded to celebrate victory and peace, and totaled up the cost—at least $32 billion in addition to 50,000 lives—Wilson set out for the Versailles Peace Conference on December 4, 1918. He was well received in France and, during the early months of 1919, worked out with his colleagues at Versailles a peace treaty that would harshly punish Germany as the aggressor in World War I and, more importantly to Wilson, establish a League of Nations where, he and his supporters hoped, disputes between nations could in the future be settled by peaceful negotiations. It did not work out as Wilson hoped. Though he planned to take his treaty and plans for the League of Nations to the American people, Wilson faced the determined opposition of a powerful group of Republicans led by Henry Cabot Lodge of Massachusetts in the Senate, which had the power to ratify or reject the treaty. Lodge's group felt that in joining the League, America would be giving up too much political independence and freedom of action. Wilson's health collapsed disastrously during his speaking tour in support of his policy, and the Senate rejected the treaty and the League of Nations on November 19, 1919.

■ **Armistice Day, 1918** *(left),* a scene of celebration that was duplicated in cities and small towns across the United States when the fighting stopped on November 11.

■ Songwriter **Irving Berlin** *(left)*, born in Russia in 1888, author of countless American standards such as "Alexander's Ragtime Band," "Easter Parade," "White Christmas," and the scores of many Broadway and Hollywood musicals including *Annie Get Your Gun* (1946), is shown here in the offices of a New York City music publisher in the 1920s. Berlin wrote "God Bless America" for his 1918 musical *Yip, Yip, Yaphank,* but the song was withdrawn from the show before it opened. Resurrected by singer Kate Smith on her radio program in 1938, it became one of the songs most associated with Berlin's memory. He died in 1989 at the age of 101.

■ **Charlie Chaplin** *(below)* and the four-year old Jackie Coogan as they appeared in Chaplin's 1921 classic, *The Kid,* the film which launched Coogan's career as a child star. The greatest actor of film's silent era, Chaplin—who continued to act in pantomime after sound was introduced—came from a background in English vaudeville to write, direct, and perform in such unforgettable films as *The Gold Rush* (1925), *City Lights* (1931), and *Modern Times* (1936), a major success for Chaplin and co-star Paulette Goddard though made as a silent after sound had taken over Hollywood. Chaplin finally spoke on the screen in his memorable and timely political satire *The Great Dictator* (1940).

■ **George M. Cohan** photographed with his parents and sister *(left)* with whom he performed on stage before the turn of the century. Born in 1878, Cohan was a versatile theatrical talent—actor, singer, playwright, song writer and producer. He is best remembered today for having written such standard songs as "You're A Grand Old Flag" and "Over There," of World War I fame, and "Give My Regards to Broadway." His career was the subject of Jimmy Cagney's immortal 1942 screen performance in *Yankee Doodle Dandy,* released the year Cohan died.

■ **George Washington Carver** *(top, left)* in his laboratory at Alabama's Tuskegee Institute. Born a slave about the time the Civil War was starting, Carver persisted in his search for education and received bachelors and masters degrees in agricultural science from Simpson College in Indianola, Iowa in 1894 and 1896. He left Iowa for Booker T. Washington's Tuskegee Institute to head its Dept. of Agriculture, where he remained until his death in 1943. Carver's years there were devoted to the research which led to the development of more than 300 food and industrial products—from flour to ink, cosmetics and wood stains—made from peanuts and over 100 from sweet potatoes.

■ Chicago White Sox outfielder **"Shoeless" Joe Jackson** *(top, center),* shown here at bat during 1920, his final season in major-league baseball. Playing thirteen seasons with Philadelphia, Cleveland, and finally the White Sox, Jackson compiled some impressive statistics; his .356 career batting average is third on the all-time list behind Ty Cobb and Rogers Hornsby. His career ended abruptly as one of the eight 'Black Sox' banned from the game for life by Commissioner Kenesaw Mountain Landis after the 1920 season for having intentionally lost the 1919 World Series to Cincinnati in a betting scheme orchestrated by a well-known New York gambler, Arnold Rothstein.

■ Composer **George Gershwin** *(top, right)* at his piano c. 1930. Gershwin packed an enormous amount of composing into little more than twenty years between his first successful songs—including "Swanee," his first major hit, sung by Al Jolson in the Broadway show *Sinbad* during the 1918–1919 season—and his untimely death in 1937, two months short of his 39th birthday. The year 1924 was climactic for Gershwin; it saw the success on Broadway of the first of many musicals, *Lady Be Good,* in which he collaborated with his lyricist brother, Ira, and the first performance of his major orchestral jazz work, *Rhapsody in Blue.* Gershwin's masterpiece, the opera *Porgy and Bess,* opened in 1935. Innumerable songs written by George with lyrics by Ira—"Fascinating Rhythm," "The Man I Love," "They Can't Take That Away From Me" are just a few examples—have achieved the status of American standards.

■ A photographic portrait of **Albert Einstein** *(right)* from the years after he arrived in the United States in 1933 as a refugee from Hitler's Germany to join the Institute for Advanced Study in Princeton, New Jersey, where he lived until his death in 1955. He became a U.S. citizen in 1940. In 1939, Einstein wrote to President Roosevelt alerting him to the potential military danger posed by the possibility that Germany might produce a workable atomic bomb first. The Manhattan Project was organized as a result of Einstein's letter.

■ **Mary Pickford** *(top left),* the silent screen's leading lady, in a 1919 photograph taken when she was at the height of her popularity as "America's sweetheart." Born in Toronto in 1893, Pickford began as a stage actress, appearing on Broadway under her real name, Gladys Mary Smith. Her first film roles were for D.W. Griffith's Biograph Studio, and she starred in his 1909 film *The Lonely Villa.* Later films included *Rebecca of Sunnybrook Farm* (1917), *Poor Little Rich Girl* (1917), and *Pollyanna* (1920). In 1919 she joined Griffith, Charlie Chaplin and Douglas Fairbanks in founding United Artists. She retired from making movies in the early 1930s, and died in 1979 at the age of 86.

■ Supreme Court Justice **Oliver Wendell Holmes, Jr.** *(top center),* a member of the Court from 1902, when he was appointed by President Theodore Roosevelt, until he retired in 1932. Son of physician, poet, and essayist Oliver Wendell Holmes, Sr., Holmes was born in 1841, and served in the Civil War as a member of the 20th Massachusetts Regiment of Volunteers before undertaking his career in the law. He taught at Harvard, wrote his classic *The Common Law* (1881), and served on the Supreme Judicial Court of Massachusetts before joining the U.S. Supreme Court at the age of 61. During his thirty years on the nation's highest court, Holmes proved to be a great defender of American civil liberties and advocate of the principle of judicial restraint. He died in 1935.

■ An exhausted dancer supported by her partner at a **dance marathon** *(top right),* a new fad popular in the 1920s and 1930s. Couples competed to see who could stay on their feet the longest, and some marathons went on for days before winners emerged. An occasional death from exhaustion provoked unfavorable newspaper comment, but the fad, like many others, more or less died out by itself.

■ **Margaret Gorman** *(left),* the sixteen-year-old winner of the first "Miss America" beauty pageant, receiving the key to the city from Atlantic City's mayor after her victory over five other contestants on September 7, 1921. Conceived by local businessmen as an attraction to keep tourists in Atlantic City after Labor Day, the Miss America contest went on to become an American institution.

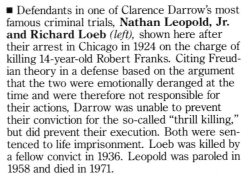

■ Defendants in one of Clarence Darrow's most famous criminal trials, **Nathan Leopold, Jr. and Richard Loeb** *(left),* shown here after their arrest in Chicago in 1924 on the charge of killing 14-year-old Robert Franks. Citing Freudian theory in a defense based on the argument that the two were emotionally deranged at the time and were therefore not responsible for their actions, Darrow was unable to prevent their conviction for the so-called "thrill killing," but did prevent their execution. Both were sentenced to life imprisonment. Loeb was killed by a fellow convict in 1936. Leopold was paroled in 1958 and died in 1971.

■ **Clarence Darrow and William Jennings Bryan** *(left),* rival lawyers chatting in the courtroom where in a near-carnival atmosphere the Scopes trial was held in Dayton, Tennessee, July 10–21, 1925. Darrow, defense lawyer in many of the memorable criminal trials of this century, had first made his mark defending labor leaders such as Eugene V. Debs (unsuccessfully in a contempt of court case during the 1894 Pullman Strike) and "Big Bill" Haywood (successfully on a charge of assassinating the former Governor of Idaho Frank R. Steunenberg). John T. Scopes was a high school teacher who was charged with breaking a Tennessee law by teaching the Darwinian theory of evolution. Bryan was selected as prosecutor because of his position as a spokesman for Biblical fundamentalism. The most dramatic moments of the trial came when Darrow called Bryan as an expert witness on the Bible and grilled him unmercifully on the scientific meaning of the scriptures. Though Bryan wilted under fire, Scopes was convicted; five days after the trial ended Bryan died of a cerebral hemorrhage.

■ **The Teapot Dome scandal** *(below)* rocked the presidency of Republican Warren Gamaliel Harding, who had been elected in 1920. Named for the Wyoming oil fields reserved for the use of the Navy, Teapot Dome came to be synonymous with corruption at the highest levels of the federal government during the carefree and irresponsible decade of the 1920s. As was learned during lengthy Congressional investigations, Harding's Secretary of the Interior, Albert B. Fall, had been bribed to issue, on very favorable terms, leases for the Teapot Dome oil fields, as well as some California oil reserves, to Harry F. Sinclair—on the right, with his attorneys, in this photograph—of the Mammoth Oil Company and Edward L. Doheny of Pan American Petroleum. When the scandal became public, the leases were cancelled, Fall resigned and was eventually fined $100,000 and imprisoned for a year, but Doheny and Sinclair were acquitted. Harding, who had early expressed confidence in Fall, but had finally been forced to condemn him, died in office in 1923 while Teapot Dome was still being investigated.

■ **Bill Tilden** *(right),* the dominant male tennis player of the 1920s, in action at Forest Hills, New York in 1926, the year his streak of six consecutive U.S. singles championships came to an end. After three years out of the winner's circle, Tilden came back to take the U.S. championship for the seventh and last time in 1929. Tilden was also the first American man to win the singles title at Wimbledon, with victories there in 1920, 1921, and 1930. Handsome, impeccably dressed, with an overpowering game and mastery of strategy and tactics, Tilden was to tennis what Babe Ruth was to baseball, Bobby Jones to golf, and Red Grange to football during the flamboyant 1920s.

■ Contralto **Marian Anderson** *(left),* whose rise as a concert performer broke many barriers for black artists in the first half of this century. Born in Philadelphia, Anderson began her singing career as a child in the choir of the Union Baptist Church. In 1925 she won a contest which earned her a performance with the New York Philharmonic. After several successful tours in Europe, Anderson returned to New York in 1935. When, in 1939, she was blocked on racial grounds from singing at Washington's Constitution Hall by the Daughters of the American Revolution, Eleanor Roosevelt and others arranged an alternative concert which drew a crowd of 75,000 at the Lincoln Memorial. Roosevelt then resigned her membership in the D.A.R. Anderson was the first black to perform with New York's Metropolitan Opera, making her dubut there in 1955 as Ulrica in Verdi's *Un ballo in maschera.* Toscanini once said that Anderson had the kind of voice that comes along once in a hundred years. She published her autobiography, *My Lord, What A Morning,* in 1957.

■ **The Ku Klux Klan** *(above)* parading in Washington, D.C. in 1925. The original Ku Klux Klan was founded in Tennessee after the Civil War to oppose the efforts of Radical Reconstructionists in the Old South. Through violence and intimidation, the Klan fought for white supremacy, and sought to avoid sharing political power with newly-enfranchised blacks. Congress reacted with various acts to try to oppose the power of the Klan and related groups, but was hardly successful. Local Klan groups remained active and violent long after the original organization had officially disbanded itself in 1869. As the power of Reconstructionist governments faded later in the century, however, and political power in the South returned to the Democratic Party, the power and activities of the Klan faded for a time. The 20th-century version of the Klan was a new organization, founded by the Rev. William Simmonds near Atlanta, Georgia in 1915. Peaking in power in the 1920s, but continuing strong into the 1930s and beyond, the Klan, still with the white hooded robes and other regalia seen in this photograph, continued to oppose civil and political rights for blacks, and added to that agenda opposition to Roman Catholics, Jews, foreigners generally, and organized labor. Standing for the political power of white Protestant Southerners, the Klan continued to influence events by violent and illegal methods. After declining again in the later 1930s, the Klan resurrected itself in the 1960s in opposition to the Civil Rights Act of 1964. In 1965, President Johnson denounced the Klan in a nationwide television address.

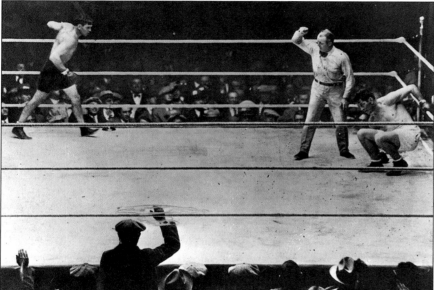

■ **Rudolph Valentino** *(left, top)* with Agnes Ayres in their 1921 classic *The Sheik*. Born in Italy in 1895, Valentino came to the United States in 1913 and worked at a variety of jobs before arriving in Hollywood in 1918. He became a star in *The Four Horsemen of the Apocalypse* (1921). In the first half of the 1920s, he was Hollywood's embodiment of the swashbuckling romantic leading man, his film roles including *Blood and Sand* (1922), *The Eagle* (1925), and *The Son of the Sheik* (1926). His death on August 23, 1926, caused by a perforated ulcer, was devasting to his fans around the world.

■ Perhaps the most famous moment in the history of heavyweight boxing, the seventh round of the second **Jack Dempsey–Gene Tunney** fight *(left, middle)*—the "Long Count" fight—at Chicago's Soldiers Field on September 22, 1927. In this photograph, champion Gene Tunney is seen at right rising as referee Dave Barry continues his count, while challenger Jack Dempsey leaves the corner at left to resume the fight. Seconds earlier, Dempsey, after knocking Tunney down, had stood over his fallen opponent in violation of the rules requiring him to go to a neutral corner. The referee delayed the count for five or six seconds until Dempsey moved toward the neutral corner. Added to the count of nine which Tunney took, the extra seconds certainly aided his recovery. The well-trained Tunney came back to win the fight by a ten-round decision.

■ The marquee of Warner's Theatre in New York City in 1927 advertising **Al Jolson** in ***The Jazz Singer*** *(above)*, the first full-length film to combine music, sound effects and synchronized speech. The success of *The Jazz Singer* effectively ended the silent film era. Jolson, born Asa Yoelson in Lithuania in 1886, emigrated to the United States in 1893. Raised in Washington, D.C., he began in vaudeville, and conquered New York as a singer on Broadway in the years before and after World War I. After *The Jazz Singer*, the dynamic Jolson went on to many other film successes, including *The Singing Fool* (1928), *Hallelujah, I'm a Bum* (1933), and *Swanee River* (1940). He died in 1950.

■ **The first practical demonstration of television in the United States,** April 7, 1927 *(left, bottom)*. Herbert Hoover, then Secretary of Commerce, is shown here speaking from his office in Washington, D.C.; he was seen and heard by A.T.&T. President Walter S. Gifford in New York, as their voices and images were carried between their offices by telephone wires.

■ The murder trial in 1921, of **Nicola Sacco and Bartolomeo Vanzetti** *(left)* provided the 1920s with a momentous *cause celebre*. Sacco and Vanzetti, immigrants from Italy and political anarchists, were arrested for the murders of a factory paymaster and a guard during a robbery in South Braintree, Massachusetts on April 20, 1920. They were found guilty the following year. Despite evidence that the trial had been prejudicially conducted, and that implicated others in the crime, the original trial judge, Webster Thayer, was able to prevent the case ever being reopened. Worldwide protests that Sacco and Vanzetti had been railroaded because of their political beliefs and social status failed to stop their execution on August 23, 1927. The case became a rallying-point for left-wing protesters throughout the 1930s and beyond.

■ **Charles A. Lindbergh** *(right),* standing in front of his Wright-powered Ryan monoplane, *Spirit of St. Louis,* on May 31, 1927, ten days after he had completed the first solo, nonstop, transatlantic flight. The airplane was named for Lindbergh's sponsorship by a group of St. Louis businessmen in a contest to win a $25,000 prize for the first nonstop flight from New York to Paris. Navigating by dead reckoning, Lindbergh flew the 3,600 miles from Roosevelt Field, Long Island to Le Bourget Field outside Paris in 33 hours, 39 minutes. After his solo flight to Paris, little happened to Lindbergh for the rest of his life that wasn't newsworthy. In one of the 1930s most famous crime stories, Lindbergh's infant son was kidnapped and murdered in 1932, a crime for which a German immigrant Bruno Hauptmann was convicted on circumstantial evidence, and executed in 1936. In the late 1930s, Lindbergh was an advocate of U.S. neutrality in World War II, a stance which drew criticism from President Franklin D. Roosevelt and many others. Though he resigned his Air Corps Reserve commission in 1941 because of this controversy, Lindbergh went on to serve as a consultant to the aviation industry during the war, and also flew 50 combat missions in the Pacific. He died in 1974.

■ American anthropologist **Margaret Mead** *(left, top),* in 1928 at the time her first major work, *Coming Of Age in Samoa,* was published. Mead pursued interests in many cultures, especially in customs and attitudes concerning childhood and adolescence, the conditioning of sexual behavior, and the development of national character. Her published works, many of which reached a wide popular audience included *Male and Female* (1949), *Culture and Commitment* (1970), and an autobiography of her early life, *Blackberry Winter* (1972). She died in 1976.

■ **The St. Valentine's Day Massacre** *(left, bottom)* of members of Chicago's "Bugs" Moran gang, who were killed in a Chicago garage on February 14, 1929 by members of Al Capone's rival organization. The killing of seven unarmed bootleggers by their rivals, disguised as policemen, typified the violence of Chicago during Prohibition as rival gangs clashed over territory. The country gradually turned away from Prohibition, both because it obviously didn't work and because of the criminal activity it seemed to encourage. Franklin Roosevelt's 1932 Democratic Party Platform called for repeal, and with his landslide victory Prohibition was doomed.

■ **Johnny Weissmuller** *(below),* star sprinter on the United States' Olympic swimming team, and winner of gold medals at the 1924 Paris Olympics in the 100-meter freestyle and the 400-meter freestyle. Weissmuller successfully defended his 100-meter title with another gold medal at the 1928 Amsterdam summer games. He then parlayed his good looks and the recognition he had achieved into a successful career playing Tarzan in the movies.

■ One of the last photographs taken of the homespun Western humorist **Will Rogers** *(top left)* before he was killed with famed pilot Wiley Post in an airplane crash on August 15, 1935 near Point Barrow, Alaska. Born in 1879 in the Indian Territory which later became Oklahoma, Rogers entered show business with a rope twirling and lassoing act in wild west shows. In 1915, in Ziegfeld's *Midnight Frolic* on stage in New York, Rogers introduced the irreverent political humor which became his trademark. "I am a member of no organized political party," began a typical Rogers quip, "I am a Democrat." In the 1920s Rogers sharpened his humor in a syndicated newspaper column which led to several successful books.

■ A 1922 photograph of **Robert Tyre "Bobby" Jones** *(top right),* the amateur golfer who dominated the sport in the 1920s. Winner of the U.S. Open four times—1923, 1926, 1929, and 1930—Jones completed the first golf "Grand Slam" when he won in a single year, 1930, the four major titles of his era, the Open and Amateur championships of both Great Britain and the United States. An Atlanta attorney who never played professional golf, Jones largely retired from championship play at the age of 28 after his 1930 U.S. Amateur victory.

■ **Signal Hill Oil Fields** *(bottom),* Long Beach, California, a 1929 photograph that illustrates how quickly the face of the nation changed in the automotive-industrial age which, beginning in the last third of the 19th century, made oil a major concern and, for some, a major source of wealth. Only a few decades before, California had been an undiscovered wilderness, accessible only by a long sea journey or a trip by covered wagon across two thousand miles of prairies and mountains; now here were forests of man-made oil wells stretching farther than the eye could see.

■ Black Tuesday on Wall Street
(top), October 29, 1929, the worst day
in the history of the stock market, continuing the steep decline in stock prices
which had begun the week before on
"Black Thursday," the day the crash began. The financial debacle marked the
end of the Roaring Twenties and the
start of the Great Depression. As the
dismal news from the nation's largest financial market deepened throughout the
day, the crowds outside in the street got
bigger and bigger. While the stories of
brokers and investors jumping out of
windows are surely largely apocryphal,
the crash was real. Within two weeks of
the 1929 stock market crash, the value
of U.S. securities declined by $30 bil-
lion. While the Administration of President Herbert Hoover, secure in their
belief that the economy was fundamentally sound and that Wall Street had just
seen a little "distress selling," urged
people to stay calm, others realized that
a major crisis was at hand.

■ A bread line *(bottom)* during the
Depression. Conditions, which worsened for a few years after the 1929
crash in America, were equally bad in
Western Europe, as economic activity
universally declined and world trade fell
to half its pre-crash value. In 1930, with
the stock market still declining, President Hoover both backed a modest ap-
propriation for an emergency job
program and signed the Smoot-Hawley
Tariff law, the highest tariff on imported
goods in the nation's history, in an effort
to protect American workers' share of
the U.S. market. Neither accomplished
very much. By early 1931 there were
four to five million unemployed and the
consequences of what this might mean
to American society were being debated
widely.

■ **Unemployed New Yorkers** *(top)* at the New York Municipal Lodging House in 1930. By the end of 1932, three years after the stock market crash, one out of four workers in the United States was unemployed. The steel industry was operating at 12% of capacity. Five thousand banks had failed. A new class of two million vagrants roamed the country with no place to go. A "Bonus Army" of 9,000 former servicemen descended on Washington, D.C. in July, 1932 to demand immediate payment of bonuses for having served in World War I, which they were scheduled by Congress to collect in 1945; the Bonus Army was brutally dispersed by federal troops under the command of General Douglas MacArthur. With no economic hope in sight, the country turned in the fall of 1932 to the "New Deal" being offered by Democratic Presidential candidate Franklin Delano Roosevelt, then governor of New York State. Roosevelt was elected with an overwhelming majority, 23 million popular votes to 15 million for Hoover.

■ **The apple-seller's story** *(bottom)*, 1930. Roosevelt took office on March 4, 1933, and immediately issued an order temporarily closing the nation's banks to give them time to regroup. FDR's first few months in office were an active time; legislation was passed in many areas—to regulate securities, to insure bank deposits, to help farmers refinance their farms, to establish the Civilian Conservation Corps, just to name a few. The Depression continued, but there were enough hopeful signs by 1936 for FDR to be reelected with ease, carrying every state except Maine and Vermont. While the New Deal measures of Roosevelt helped put some people to work and aided others in great distress, high unemployment and poor economic conditions persisted until the end of the 1930s. Only World War II, with its demand for men, and munitions and other manufactured goods, ended the long slump and launched a new economic era.

■ **Mildred "Babe" Didrikson** *(left, top)*, the greatest woman athlete of the 1930s, demonstrating the form she used to win a gold medal in the javelin throw at the 1932 Los Angeles Olympic Games, where she also won the 80-meter hurdles. After 1934 Didrikson turned her attention to golf, winning many amateur and professional titles; in 1947 she won 17 consecutive tournaments.

■ **Cole Porter** *(left, middle)* whose elegant and sophisticated wit made him in the 1930s a leading composer for the American musical comedy stage. After an early Broadway musical, *See America First* (1916), Porter entertained French troops in North Africa, served in the U.S. military in 1917–18, and traveled widely in Europe in the 1920s, spending some time studying with French composer Vincent d'Indy. Back on Broadway, Porter rose to the top with such shows as *Fifty Million Frenchmen* (1929), *The Gay Divorcee* (1932), and *Anything Goes* (1934). Later productions included *Kiss Me Kate* (1948), *Can-Can* (1953), and *Silk Stockings* (1955). Among the vast number of popular standards which epitomize his uniquely urbane style are songs such as "I Get A Kick Out Of You," "Begin the Beguine," "In the Still of the Night," and "You're The Top."

■ A workman taking a break during the construction of the **Empire State Building** *(above)* which was completed in 1931 at Fifth Avenue and 34th Street on the site of the original Waldorf-Astoria Hotel. The top of the Chrysler Building may be seen in the background. When it opened, the Empire State Building was, at 1,245 feet, the world's tallest. It was designed by the architectural firm of Shreve, Lamb and Harrison to include a landing mast for dirigibles, an idea that proved unfeasible because of the city's erratic air currents. Television antennas instead have been used to take advantage of the Empire State Building's height.

■ One of the many infamous incidents of **racial lynching in the 1930s** *(left, bottom)*—blacks Abram Smith (on the left) and Thomas Shipp, hanged in the public square in Marion, Indiana on August 9, 1930 after a huge mob had taken them from the county jail. Smith and Shipp had been accused of murdering a white man and his girl friend. Between 1882, the first year for which there are records, and 1951, 4,730 Americans, of whom 3,437 were black, were lynched. At the end of 1952, Alabama's Tuskegee Institute reported that the country had just completed the first year since 1881 when no lynchings were reported anywhere in the United States. During those decades, anti-lynching laws prescribing federal penalties for law enforcement officials who allowed mob justice to operate—often in the guise of the Ku Klux Klan—were routinely defeated in the U.S. Senate by Southern filibusters. The origin of the term *lynching* is obscure, though some have traced it to a Virginia planter during the American Revolution named Charles Lynch who organized an unsanctioned court which targeted British loyalists.

■ The infamous **Bonnie Parker and Clyde Barrow** *(above left)* clowning for the camera in a photograph taken not too long before their luck ran out and both were killed in a gunfight with police near the town of Ruston, Louisiana on May 23, 1934. For a few years Parker and Barrow had roamed the Mississippi Valley, holding up banks and gas stations and killing 12 people. Their epitaph was written by John Dillinger: "They're punks. They're giving bank-robbing a bad name."

■ **Shirley Temple** *(above right)*, the singing, dancing quintessential child star of the 1930s. In 1934, after a series of screen successes which included *Stand Up and Cheer, Little Miss Marker,* and *Bright Eyes*—the film in which she sang "On the Good Ship Lollipop"—Temple was suddenly the leading box-office attraction in Hollywood. The next few years saw additional hit films including *Wee Willie Winkie* (1937) and *The Little Princess* (1939). By 1940, the year she turned twelve, Temple's childhood and her reign in Hollywood were coming to the end; her later efforts in film and television, while not unsuccessful, did not match her classic movies. As a prominent member of California's Republican Party, Temple went on in later years to a new career as a diplomat. As Shirley Temple Black, she served as a United States delegate to the United Nations General Assembly in 1969–70, was ambassador to Ghana in 1974–76, chief of protocol in the White House in 1976–77, and she is currently U.S. ambassador to Czechoslovakia.

■ **Eugene O'Neill** *(above center),* who in 1936 became the only American playwright to win the Nobel Prize for Literature. This photograph was taken in 1926 in Bermuda, where O'Neill had a home, when he was approaching the height of his fame as America's leading dramatist. The son of a prominent actor, O'Neill won a Pulitzer Prize in 1920 for his first full-length play, *Beyond the Horizon.* Later major works include *Strange Interlude* (1928), *The Iceman Cometh* (1946), and *Long Day's Journey Into Night,* published three years after his death in 1953.

■ **Fred Astaire and Ginger Rogers** *(right),* in a scene from their 1936 movie *Pick Yourself Up.* After dancing as a child star in vaudeville and later on Broadway in the 1920s, Astaire made his film debut in *Dancing Lady* in 1933, the year that saw the first of his film collaborations—*Flying Down to Rio*—with dance partner Rogers. The Astaire-Rogers team produced a wildly successful series of films which included *Top Hat, Swing Time,* and *The Story of Vernon and Irene Castle.* Astaire and Rogers portrayed the sophisticated side of the 1930s, providing wonderful escapist entertainment during the depths of the Depression. Their films revolutionized the movie musical comedy through their mastery of technical detail—a major factor was Astaire's insistence that their whole bodies should always be shown while dancing to prove that technical trickery was not being substituted for the real thing—and their consummate integration of music, dance, and plot.

■ **A dust storm on the plains** *(top left)* in 1937. Farmers and ranchers of the Middle West and Plains states not only had to contend with the Depression in the 1930s, but by the middle of the decade the vast area had been transformed into what came to be called the Dust Bowl—six consecutive years of drought ravaged the once-fertile farm land, eroding vital topsoil, leaving cattle with nothing but dirt to eat, and exposing farms and towns to clouds of dust like the one in this photograph. Major dust storms began in Texas and Oklahoma in 1933, and eventually had an impact on the whole Midwest.

■ **A California migrant family,** *(middle),* photographed in 1936 in Nipomo, California by Dorothea Lange for the Farm Security Administration. Thousands of farmers who couldn't survive in the Oklahoma dust bowl headed west in the 1930s, hoping to find new homes in California or the Pacific Northwest—this was the background of John Steinbeck's classic fictional account, *The Grapes of Wrath* (1939)—only to discover that there was no work for them except as migrant laborers.

■ **A grasshopper plague in South Dakota** *(above),* a photograph taken on July 10, 1936 in Miller, South Dakota. This farmer can only watch his property, already virtually destroyed by years of drought, now beset by a plague of grasshoppers covering everything in sight.

■ **President Franklin Delano Roosevelt** *(bottom),* in a characteristic pose, in the summer of 1937 during the first year of his second administration. After his landslide victory over Alf Landon in 1936, Roosevelt's attention turned more toward foreign affairs as Europe moved toward the seemingly inevitable start of another World War. The domestic policies of the New Deal continued, and were developed and expanded, but true economic recovery proved elusive. Whatever his political problems at home, Roosevelt, unwilling to consider retirement with war on the horizon, went on in 1940 to win the presidency for an unprecedented third term. The margin of victory over Republican Wendell Wilkie was Roosevelt's narrowest yet, but still a decisive 27 million popular votes to 22 million. Roosevelt interpreted his reelection as a mandate to proceed with his Lend-Lease support of Britain, already at war with Germany. In 1944, with World War II nearing its end, Roosevelt would win his final presidential election, over Thomas E. Dewey, by a still narrower margin, and would serve only a few months of his final term before his death on April 12, 1945.

■ **Two giants of jazz** *(left)*, clarinetist **Benny Goodman** and drummer **Gene Krupa,** photographed in 1938, the year Krupa left Goodman's band to form his own. Both were born in Chicago in 1909, and both got their starts with early Chicago jazz bands. In 1934 Goodman formed the band that made him a legend as "The King of Swing." For the next decade and a half, American popular music was dominated by the sound of the classic "Big Bands" led by Goodman, Krupa, Tommy and Jimmy Dorsey, Artie Shaw, Glenn Miller, and their peers.

■ Millionaire industrialist **Howard Hughes** *(below left)*, photographed in 1936 at Chicago's Municipal Airport. In 1935, flying a plane he had designed, Hughes established a new world's record speed of 352.46 miles per hour. Three years later in a Lockheed 14, Hughes circled the earth in a then record 91 hours, 14 minutes. One of the last chapters in his career as an aviator was the design and construction of the *Spruce Goose,* the world's largest plane, an eight-engine wooden flying boat with a projected capacity of 750 passengers. Near Los Angeles on November 2, 1947, Hughes piloted the *Spruce Goose* for one mile—its only flight. Hughes's fascinating career as an industrialist, movie producer (he introduced Jean Harlow, Paul Muni, and Jane Russell to the screen), aviator, financier and storied recluse provided enough material during and after his lifetime for an army of biographers and one memorable hoax in 1971 concerning memoirs found to have been concocted by a journalist. Hughes lived in seclusion after 1950, and died in 1976.

■ American sprinter **Jesse Owens** *(below center)*, receiving the baton in a relay race at the 1936 summer Olympic Games in Berlin. With gold medals in the 100- and 200-meter sprints, the long jump and the 400-meter relay, Owens dominated the Games to the chagrin of frequent spectator Adolf Hitler, whose theory of Aryan superiority hardly accounted for a black man being the world's greatest athlete.

■ **Amelia Earhart** *(below)*, who on May 20–21, 1932 became the first woman to fly solo across the Atlantic. Flying a Pratt & Whitney Wasp-powered Lockheed Vega, she flew from Harbor Grace, Newfoundland to Londonderry, Ireland in 15 hours and 39 minutes. Three years later Earhart was the first to fly solo between Honolulu and California. On July 2, 1937, she and her copilot, Frederick J. Noonan, disappeared in the South Pacific between New Guinea and Howland Island during an attempted flight around the world.

■ The completed twin towers of the
Golden Gate Bridge *(top),* photographed
from the San Francisco side in June, 1935
with two anchorage pylons under construction in the foreground. The towers, 746
feet high, would hold the twin cables of the
bridge's 4,200-foot main span. Connecting
San Francisco and Marin County, the
Golden Gate Bridge—made of 100,000
tons of steel and 80,000 miles of wire
cable—was the longest suspension bridge
in the world from its completion in 1937 until the building of the Verrazano Narrows
Bridge in New York in 1964. Many engineering problems were overcome during its
construction—which claimed eleven
workers killed in accidents—including
blasting rock in deep water to build
earthquake-proof foundations. Two hundred
thousand people walked across the bridge
on the day it opened, May 27, 1937.

■ The dirigible **Hindenburg** *(bottom)*
bursting into flames while being secured to
a mooring tower at the Lakehurst, New
Jersey Naval Air Station in the early evening of May 6, 1937. The *Hindenburg*
made ten successful round trips between
Germany and America in 1936, her first
year in service, and had just completed the
transatlantic crossing in 60 hours from
Hamburg when her seven million cubic feet
of highly flammable hydrogen exploded
from unknown causes. Thirty-five of the
ninety-seven passengers and crew on
board, and one ground worker, were killed,
and the brief era of passenger travel by dirigible came to an abrupt end. By coinci-
dence, the disaster was heard around the
country on the nation's first coast-to-coast
live radio broadcast. Millions of stunned lis-
teners heard Herbert Morrison, an announcer with WLS in Chicago, describe the
explosion in shocked and graphic terms.

■ A vintage year for Hollywood, 1939 saw such classics as *Beau Geste, Dark Victory, Goodbye, Mr. Chips, Mr. Smith Goes To Washington, Stagecoach, Wuthering Heights,* and **The Wizard of Oz** *(right, top)*, perhaps the most successful film version of a classic children's story ever produced on the screen. Starring Jack Haley as the Tin Woodman, Ray Bolger as the Scarecrow, Judy Garland as Dorothy, and veteran Bert Lahr as the Cowardly Lion, *The Wizard* became one of Hollywood's perennial classics.

■ Max Schmeling, hanging on the ropes, as **Joe Louis** *(below left)* closes in to score his first-round knockout in their second fight, June 22, 1938 at Yankee Stadium. Louis, who had won the heavyweight title from James J. Braddock with an 8th-round knockout in Chicago exactly one year earlier, was avenging a previous loss to Schmeling, one of only three defeats in Louis's professional career. Schmeling's loss, a propaganda blow to Hitler's Germany, was wildly cheered in black neighborhoods in the United States where Louis was king. Louis held the heavyweight championship longer than any other fighter, from his victory over Braddock in 1937 until his retirement in 1949. During his tenure he successfully defended his title 25 times, winning 21 by knockout. Always willing to take on any available challenger, Louis fought competition that was sometimes so thin that sportswriters began to refer to the "Bum-of-the-Month-Club," but his title defenses also included such memorable battles as his two victories over Billy Conn. An attempt to come out of retirement and regain his title ended when he lost a 15-round decision to Ezzard Charles on September 27, 1950. In his last major fight, Louis was knocked out by Rocky Marciano in the 8th round on October 26, 1951. He died in 1981.

■ Despite all the other memorable productions, the movie event of 1939 was the December 15th premiere at Atlanta's Loew's Grand, decorated with a false front to resemble a southern mansion, of David O. Selznick's **Gone With the Wind** *(right, middle)* starring Clark Gable and Vivien Leigh. The filming of the Pulitzer-Prize winning novel by Margaret Mitchell, which had set a record of its own by selling a million hardcover copies in six months after its 1936 publication, was one of the most highly publicized events in Hollywood's history, from the search for the actress to play Scarlett O'Hara, to solving the logistics of shooting the burning of Atlanta. The result was a triumph for Selznick and his stars, as *Gone With the Wind* won Academy Awards for best picture, director (Victor Fleming), and actress (Leigh), while in a supporting role Hattie McDaniel became the first black actress to win an Oscar.

■ The 700-foot triangular **Trylon and the Perisphere** *(right, bottom)* make a futuristic display—the Perisphere housed a representation of what scientists conceived life would be like in 2036—at the opening of the New York World's Fair, as seen in this picture photographed from a television screen on the day the Fair opened, April 30, 1939. With this broadcast, which included FDR's opening remarks, making him the first President to appear on television, the National Broadcasting Company inaugurated the first regular television service to the American public. 1939 was a major year for television firsts. On April 17, NBC broadcast the first sporting event on television, a college baseball game between Columbia and Princeton with Bill Stern announcing—even though there were then only 400 sets in operation to receive it. Later that summer, Red Barber announced the first major league game on television, between the Dodgers and the Reds, from Brooklyn's Ebbets Field.

■ A Depression legend, folk singer **Woody Guthrie** *(opposite, top center),* composer of "This Land Is Your Land" and more than 1,000 other songs, many of which speak of the struggles of common people, the dispossessed and the labor movement. Born in Oklahoma in 1912, Guthrie traveled across the country during the Depression, singing and writing such songs as "Hard Traveling" and "Blowing Down This Old Dusty Road." He served in the Merchant Marine in World War II, published an autobiography, *Bound for Glory,* in 1943, and died in 1967 after a long battle with Huntington's chorea, a degenerative disease of the nervous system. His son Arlo Guthrie wrote one of the classic songs of the anti-Vietnam War Movement, "Alice's Restaurant" (1969).

■ A still from Orson Welles's classic 1941 film **Citizen Kane** *(top).* Welles's mastery of filmmaking technique made *Citizen Kane* one of the most influential movies ever made. Born in Wisconsin in 1915, Welles began acting in Dublin in the early 1930s, before returning to the United States to tour with Katherine Cornell's company in 1933–34. Later in the 1930s, Welles directed an all-black cast in *Macbeth* for the Negro People's Theatre and founded the Mercury Theatre; in 1938 his Mercury players caused a memorable but short-lived panic when their radio broadcast based on H.G. Wells's *War of the Worlds,* designed to simulate a newscast, was taken seriously. After going to Hollywood in 1940, Welles wrote, directed, and acted in many memorable films, including *The Magnificent Ambersons* (1942), *The Lady from Shanghai* (1947), and *Chimes at Midnight* (1966).

■ Novelist **Ernest Hemingway** *(opposite, top right),* photographed on a 1940s hunting trip. Born in Oak Park, Illinois in 1899, Hemingway served with the Red Cross in World War I, and began writing as a reporter with the *Kansas City Star.* A leading member of the colony of expatriate writers and artists who made Paris their base in the 1920s, Hemingway established his reputation with *The Sun Also Rises* (1926) and *A Farewell to Arms* (1929), the background of which derived from his World War I experiences. He consolidated his place in contemporary literature with several classic volumes of short stories published in the later 1920s and 1930s. Later novels included *For Whom The Bell Tolls* (1940) and *The Old Man and the Sea* (1952). Many of his most memorable stories are set in the Upper Peninsula of Michigan where he spent summers as a young man, and much of his other fiction is set in the exotic parts of the world he knew well—Spain, Cuba, and Africa. Hemingway won the Nobel Prize for Literature in 1954, and, in failing health, took his own life in 1961.

■ Humphrey Bogart and Ingrid Bergman in a scene from the closing episode of their classic 1942 film **Casablanca** *(bottom),* which won the 1943 Academy Award as best picture, as well as one for its director, Michael Curtiz. The film's tale of love and intrigue set against the background of North Africa in World War II, and the memorable performances of its stars, have earned it a permanent place on many film fans' lists of all-time favorites.

■ **Glenn Miller** *(opposite, top left)* and members of his trombone section. Leader of one of the classic 1940s big bands, Miller, also remembered for his signature composition, "Moonlight Serenade," as well as such hits as "String of Pearls" and "In the Mood," was a major with the Air Force Band in Europe when he disappeared on a flight to Paris from England on December 16, 1944. The tremendous success of James Stewart in *The Glenn Miller Story,* filmed in 1953, served to keep his music current for later generations.

■ This classic pose of film star **Betty Grable** *(opposite, bottom left)* was a favorite of American soldiers in World War II.

■ The Yankees' **Joe DiMaggio** *(opposite, bottom right),* hitting a single at Washington's Griffith Stadium on June 30, 1941, breaking George Sisler's nineteen-year-old record for hitting safely in consecutive games, and bringing his own streak to 42. DiMaggio would go on to hit safely in 56 consecutive games, establishing what is considered one of baseball's most untouchable records. At the end of the 1941 season, DiMaggio led the Yankees to victory over Brooklyn in the World Series, and for the second time was named the American League's Most Valuable Player.

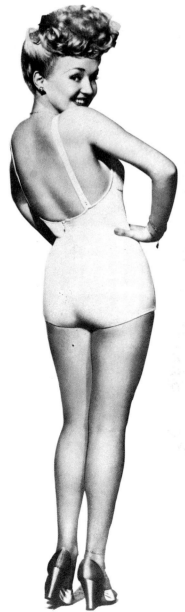

■ **Japanese families leaving the Rose Bowl** *(top)*. This photograph, taken on March 24, 1942, shows a small portion of the crowd of 1,000 Japanese-Americans who had been forced to assemble at the Rose Bowl in Pasadena, California before leaving for their "Reception Center" at Manzanar, California. In the months following the attack on Pearl Harbor, about 110,000 Japanese-Americans, two-thirds of whom had been born in the United States, were sent to internment camps, mostly in California, Arizona, Utah, Colorado and Wyoming. Under the direction of the War Relocation Authority, Japanese-American citizens were given ten days to wind up their affairs and report for internment with bed rolls and only the luggage they could carry. In recent years this policy has come to be seen as a manifestation of the hysteria of World War II's early days, a tragic overreaction uncalled for by any threat to the American war effort.

■ **The Japanese attack on Pearl Harbor** *(opposite)*, December 7, 1941, brought the United States into World War II. The battleship *U.S.S. California,* having been hit by Japanese bombers, is shown here sinking as its crew streams over the side to try to escape in small boats, a number of which are already in the water. On the far right is the tip of the hull of another sunken American battleship, the *U.S.S. Oklahoma.* The Japanese fleet under Admiral Chuichi Nagumo had approached undetected to within 275 miles north of Hawaii, and the attack by 360 fighters and bombers targeting the U.S. naval base at Pearl Harbor on Oahu Island was a complete surprise. Of the eight American battleships at Pearl Harbor, the Navy lost the *Arizona* and the *West Virginia,* in addition to the *California* and the *Oklahoma,* and the other four were damaged. Eleven other Navy ships were sunk or badly hit. Two hundred and forty-seven American planes were lost, mostly on the ground, and 2,330 military personnel and about 70 civilians were killed. The Japanese lost 28 planes. Simultaneously with the attack on Pearl Harbor, the Japanese attacked the Philippines, Guam, Hong Kong, and other targets in the Pacific. With the crippling of the American fleet at Pearl Harbor, the Japanese found themselves in control of the Pacific in the early days of the war.

■ **The front page of the *New York World-Telegram*** for December 8, 1941 *(opposite, inset)* gives an account of the previous day's attack, and details of President Roosevelt's message to Congress—"A date which will live in infamy"—and the vote of 388 to 1 in the House of Representatives and 82 to 0 in the Senate in favor of the Declaration of War against Japan. The lone dissenter in the House was Representative Jeanette Rankin of Montana, who had also voted against declaring war on Germany in 1917. Germany and Italy declared war on the United States on December 11, and on the same day Congress recognized, at Roosevelt's request, that America was at war also with those countries.

■ Newsman **Edward R. Murrow** *(bottom),* whose CBS radio broadcasts from London brought news of the early days of World War II in Europe home to America, photographed in London in 1941. Always beginning with his customary "This is London . . .," Murrow became a familiar if unseen figure in every household eager for reports from London during the tense days of the Battle of Britain in 1940 and 1941.

■ **Colonel Jimmy Doolittle** led a group of 16 B-25 Mitchell bombers, one of which is shown here *(left, top)* taking off from the aircraft carrier *Hornet,* in the North Pacific 650 miles from Japan, on April 18, 1942, just four months after the Japanese attack on Pearl Harbor. Their mission was to bomb Tokyo, and other Japanese cities. The bombing mission was a success, but though it was possible to launch the big bombers from the carrier—Doolittle's pilots had practiced intensively in Florida taking off from carrier-sized airstrips—it wasn't possible to land them. Doolittle and his men therefore continued westward after the raid. One of the planes landed in Vladivostok and was impounded by the Russians; the others flew to China, and their crews either crash-landed or bailed out. Of the 80 American crewmen who came down in China, three were killed and eight were captured. The eight prisoners were put on trial by the Chinese; five were sentenced to life in prison and three were beheaded. The Japanese were mystified as to where the bombers had come from; to preserve secrecy, the American military announced that the planes had been based at Shangri-La, the mythical country of James Hilton's bestseller, *Lost Horizons.* This isolated bombing run had no strategic impact on the course of the war, but it was a morale booster in the U.S., especially after several months of bad news from the Pacific.

■ **Navy Fighters attacking the Japanese fleet off Midway, Island** *(left, middle),* 1,000 miles west of Hawaii in the first week of June, 1942. The attack on Midway ordered by Japanese admiral Yamamoto was anticipated by the American naval command. After some unsuccessful assaults on the en-

emy fleet, the American Navy scored heavily on June 4; dive bombers from the *Enterprise* and *Yorktown* sank three Japanese heavy carriers, the *Akagi, Kaga,* and *Soryu* in one quick raid, which may have changed the entire course of the war in the five minutes it took the Japanese carriers to sink. When they were hit, all three carriers were loaded with planes about to take off, and the loss of their pilots was more devastating to the Japanese war effort than the 275 planes destroyed at Midway. Later in the battle, a fourth Japanese carrier, the *Hiryu,* was sunk. Despite the loss of the American carrier *Yorktown,* the U.S. victory at Midway was a crucial early turning point of the war, ending Japanese supremacy in the Pacific, and opening the way for the U.S. counteroffensive which began in the Solomon Islands two months later.

■ **American troops landing at Guadalcanal** *(left, bottom)* in the Solomon Islands northeast of Australia in August, 1942. This landing by the U.S. 1st Marine Division, intended to prevent the Japanese from establishing an air base there which would have hampered American efforts in the South Pacific, was the first counteroffensive against Japan. Guadalcanal saw some of the toughest combat of the war; sixteen hundred American soldiers were killed, and many times that number were disabled by malaria. After six months of hard jungle fighting, Guadalcanal was in American hands. The Japanese left behind thousands of dead, killed in action and by disease and starvation. Nine marines earned the Congressional Medal of Honor on Guadalcanal, including famed Wildcat pilot Joe Foss, who shot down 26 Japanese planes.

■ First lady **Eleanor Roosevelt** *(below)* in uniform, having just returned from an inspection trip for the Red Cross to the Pacific theatre. A niece of President Theodore Roosevelt, Eleanor married Franklin Delano Roosevelt, a distant cousin, in 1905. Beginning with his election to the New York State Senate in 1911, she was actively involved in her husband's political career, assisting him especially after he was stricken with poliomyelitis in 1921. After his inauguration as President in 1933, Eleanor Roosevelt traveled widely to gather information for FDR on the progress of his New Deal policies and, later, to help raise the morale of American troops during World War II. After FDR's death in 1945, President Truman appointed Eleanor Roosevelt, a forceful spokesperson for liberal causes, a delegate to the United Nations where she served as chairman of the U.N. Commission on Human Rights. She died in 1962.

■ American troops landing on the coast of Normandy on **D-Day June 6, 1944** *(above left)*. The long-awaited Allied invasion of the northern coast of Europe, following successful operations against the Germans and their allies in North Africa and Italy, started the final push of the war. Operation "Overlord," as the D-Day invasion was designated, was under the command of General Dwight Eisenhower from SHAEF (Supreme Headquarters, Allied Expeditionary Forces) in London. Before the invasion, the number of Allied combat troops based in the British Isles reached eight hundred thousand. A hundred and fifty thousand landed the first day on a fifty mile stretch of the coast of Normandy west from Caen, the greatest amphibious operation in military history. Four thousand ships were involved, and over ten thousand aircraft, carrying men and supplies and pounding the German positions on the coast. From the five beachheads—designated west to east Utah, Omaha, Gold, Juno and Sword— established on D-Day at the cost of 2,500 lives (fewer than had been feared), the operations began which would first drive Germany from France and eventually end the war.

■ The caption of this photograph, distributed during the war for morale purposes, identified the woman shown **making a parachute** *(above center)* somewhere in New England during World War II, as a former dancer in a New York night club, Bonnie Bonness. She is shown on a parachute rigging table affixing shroud lines to the harness, one of the final steps in parachute assembly. Three and a half million American women took jobs on factory assembly lines during World War II. Very quickly the level of production thus achieved reached staggering proportions. In the two years following the attack on Pearl Harbor, for example, the U.S. produced 150,000 military airplanes.

■ **Bombers of the U.S. 8th Air Force** *(above right)* over Tours, France in July, 1944, about six weeks after D-Day. From bases in England, a daily bombing campaign was directed at military targets and especially at crucial railroads, factories, and supply centers. The Allies dropped almost three million tons of bombs on Nazi-held Europe, two-thirds of them after D-Day. In the most devastating air raid in history, on February 13–14, 1945, the British RAF and the U.S. Air Force bombed Dresden, Germany with over a thousand planes, killing an estimated 135,000 people.

■ A scene from the **air war in the Pacific** *(below left)*, a B-24 Liberator bomber heading for a Japanese target from a U.S. base in China in 1943 as suitably nicknamed fighter planes wait their turn. The bombing campaign against Japan intensified when B-29s began operating from Saipan and other bases in the Mariana Islands in 1944. The bombing attack on Tokyo by 234 American B-29s on March 9, 1945, killed with conventional bombs 83,793 people, more than the atomic bomb attack on Hiroshima later that year.

■ **American soldiers fighting street by street** in Brest, France *(below right)* in October, 1944, four months after D-Day. This photograph is unusual for a wartime action scene because it is possible to name the soldier, Lt. M.L. Selberg, leading the charge down the street. The landings on June 6, 1944 had been just the beginning of the effort needed to end the war in Europe. In the 48 days following D-Day, the Allies suffered 122,000 casualties in France, the Germans 117,000.

■ **American troops parading in Paris** (*opposite, top*) on August 29, 1944. This huge parade took two hours to pass down the Champs Elysées to the Place de la Concorde where the soldiers were greeted by General Omar Bradley and General Charles DeGaulle. With German forces retreating in disarray, Paris had been liberated on August 23–24 by an uprising of the Free French inside the city, assisted by the French 2nd Armored Division.

■ One of the most famous photographs to come out of World War II—one which earned a Pulitzer Prize at the time for photographer Joe Rosenthal—shows American Marines **raising the flag on Iwo Jima** (*opposite, bottom left*) in February, 1945. The tiny volcanic island, strategically located 700 miles south of Tokyo, was taken after an all-out assault by the 4th and 5th Marine Divisions. While there is no question that members of the 5th Division did indeed raise an American flag on Iwo Jima's Mount Suribachi after four days of tough fighting, recent research has raised questions as to whether the flag-raising depicted here was actually conducted under battle conditions.

■ **After the Battle of the Bulge** (*opposite, bottom right*), Generals Omar Bradley, Dwight Eisenhower and George Patton, survey the war damage in Bastogne, Belgium in 1945. The German counteroffensive pushed a "bulge" into the American lines in Belgium in December, 1944. With his 101st Airborne Division surrounded at Bastogne, Brigadier General Anthony MacAuliffe sent the Germans his memorably brief reply to a demand for his surrender: "Nuts." Improved weather allowed Allied air power back into action, Bastogne was held, and the Germans were gradually placed on the defensive again.

■ **General Douglas MacArthur** (*top*), wading ashore at Leyte in the Philippines during a landing there in October, 1944. MacArthur and his troops reached Luzon on January 25, 1945. By July, 1945, all of the Philippines were once more under U.S. control and MacArthur had kept his famous promise, "I shall return," made when American and Filipino troops on Corregidor Island in Manila Bay had surrendered to the Japanese on May 6, 1942.

■ **American troops from the 45th Division** (*middle*) of the Seventh Army in Nurnberg, Germany in May, 1945— waving from the dais of an arena where Hitler, Goebbels, Goering and Himmler had addressed vast audiences. Allied forces crossed the Rhine into Germany in late March; with the Russians advancing from the east, the days of Hitler's Third Reich were numbered. By late April, the Russians had Berlin surrounded, and American and British forces were less than 200 miles away. By May 1, all resistance around Berlin had been eliminated, and Hitler had committed suicide with Eva Braun. Berlin fell the following day. Leadership of the German government passed to Grand Admiral Karl Doenitz who signed the unconditional surrender at Rheims on May 7, 1945, V-E Day.

■ **Churchill, Roosevelt and Stalin** (*bottom*) at their historic meeting at Yalta in the Crimea in February, 1945. Stalin's position at the bargaining table was strong following the defeat of the German invasion of Russia. With victory in Europe now assured, the Allied leaders made plans to divide Germany after hostilities ceased and to adjust Russia's border with Poland as Stalin wished. The cost of the defeat of Nazi Germany had been immense—six million battle deaths for Russia, half that many for Germany. American dead in WWII battles totalled 291,557.

■ **Major General Leslie R. Groves,** the Army's chief of engineering on the Manhattan Project's development of the first atomic bomb, and **Dr. J.R. Oppenheimer,** Director of the Los Alamos Bomb Project, *(opposite, top left)* viewing the remains of the base of the steel tower on which the first bomb was hung for testing at Alamagordo, New Mexico on July 16, 1945. The bomb melted the tower and turned the surrounding sand into jade green glasslike cinders. Over a hundred thousand scientists, technicians, and support personnel worked at Oak Ridge, Tennessee, Hanford, Washington, and Los Alamos, New Mexico in what was considered a frantic race to create the first atomic bomb. Three weeks after this experimental atomic explosion, President Truman ordered the bombing with atomic weapons of Hiroshima and Nagasaki.

■ The battleship *U.S.S. Missouri (opposite, bottom left)* in action in 1945. While continuing to pound Japan from the air, the U.S. waged an unremitting sea war. More than eight million tons of Japanese shipping were sunk during the war, more than half by American submarines. By mid-July, 1945, the American Navy was firing guns such as those pictured here at targets in Japan from Japanese coastal waters.

■ **Victims of the bombing of Hiroshima** *(opposite, top right).* The United States demanded the surrender of Japan on July 27, 1945 with the threat that the newly-developed atomic bomb would be used if the surrender was not forthcoming. The Japanese rejected this ultimatum. On August 6, a B-29 based on Tinian, the *Enola Gay,* commanded by Col. Paul W. Tibbets, Jr., dropped a single atomic bomb with the destructive power of 20,000 tons of TNT on Hiroshima. Of Hiroshima's population of about 300,000, the bomb killed 71,379. Having received no response from the Japanese government, three days later the U.S. dropped a similar bomb on Nagasaki. On August 14, 1945, the Japanese agreed to unconditional surrender, ending the war in the Pacific.

■ August 14, 1945, **V-J day** *(opposite, bottom right),* the day the war with Japan was won, as marked in New York's Times Square at the Trans-Lux Theatre by a happy sailor and his girlfriend.

■ **The Japanese delegation aboard the *U.S.S. Missouri*** *(above),* in Tokyo harbor on September 2, 1945, to sign the formal unconditional surrender document at the end of World War II. The Allied forces were represented by General Douglas MacArthur. Given a relatively free hand in establishing Allied policy concerning defeated Japan, MacArthur rejected the idea, in the interest of maintaining peace and stability, of trying Emperor Hirohito as a war criminal.

"The unleashed power of the atom has changed everything save our modes of thinking, and we thus drift toward unparalleled catastrophes."

—ALBERT EINSTEIN

■ The Brooklyn Dodgers' **Jackie Robinson** *(top)* in 1947, the year he became the first black player in baseball's major leagues. After football stardom at UCLA, Robinson was signed by Dodgers' President Branch Rickey to a minor league contract in 1945. Despite verbal abuse and threats from those opposed to the end of baseball's color line, Robinson played his first major league game on April 11, 1947. Named the National League's Most Valuable Player after the 1949 season, Robinson had an outstanding ten-year career, mostly as a second baseman, which earned him admission to the Hall of Fame in 1962. Larry Doby joined the Cleveland Indians midway through the 1947 season to become the American League's first black player.

■ **Louis "Satchmo" Armstrong** *(middle)*, the greatest trumpet player in the history of jazz. Born in New Orleans on July 4, 1900, Armstrong heard many jazz pioneers on the streets of his native city. His career as a professional musician took off when he left New Orleans in 1922 to join King Oliver's Creole Jazz Band in Chicago—such memorable recordings as "Canal Street Blues" remain from this early period. In the 1920s, Armstrong performed with groups of his own such as the Hot Five and Hot Seven ensembles. His place in jazz history is linked with the rise of the virtuoso soloist, a role he popularized and perfected in the 1920s with such pieces as "Savoy Blues," "Potato Head Blues," "West End Blues," "Tiger Rag," and countless others. Armstrong became more than a musician, however—his irrepressible personality made him a universal ambassador of jazz to the world and brought him fame as a bandleader, 'scat' singer (utilizing vocal sounds as one would an instrument), comedian, and film actor. He died in 1971.

■ **A "Colored Only" general store** *(bottom)*, photographed in Belle Glade, Florida in 1945. The battle against "Jim Crow" laws providing for racial segregation at all kinds of public facilities went on in the southern states for over a century after the Civil War.

■ Dancer, choreographer, and teacher of modern dance, **Martha Graham** *(top),* captured in a classic 1945 Barbara Morgan photograph performing her ballet *Letter to the World,* based on the life of poet Emily Dickinson. A native of Pittsburgh, Graham studied with Ruth St. Denis and Ted Shawn, taught at the Eastman School of Music in Rochester, New York, and made her New York City debut in 1926. In a legendary and long career—Graham retired as a dancer in 1970 at the age of 76 and died in 1991—she created almost 150 works and performed in most of them herself.

■ **John Bardeen, William Shockley, and Walter H. Brattain** *(middle),* three American scientists whose work transformed American life, shown here in a 1948 photograph at the Bell Labs in Murray Hill, New Jersey when their invention of the transistor was announced. The transistor, a tiny metal disk which amplifies electric current without a heated filament, revolutionized the electronics industry and with it the business, personal, and recreational lives of almost every American. The trio shared the 1956 Nobel Prize in Physics for their work on the transistor; Bardeen went on to share another Nobel in 1972 for his work in superconductivity.

■ West Berliners responding to an American plane overhead during the **Berlin Airlift** *(bottom)* of 1948–49, a major episode of the early years of the Cold War. Using as a pretext the Western powers' decision to unite their occupied German zones into a single economic unit, the Russians declared the four-power administration of Berlin over, and began a blockade of all water, road, and rail communication between Berlin and the west in the late spring of 1948. On June 26, 1948, the United States and Britain began the airlift to supply West Berlin's vital needs. As the airlift continued, military and political tensions rose and both sides sent impressive reinforcements to the area. The airlift continued for over a year, overcoming many logistical difficulties, and supplying West Berlin with over two million tons of food and other essential supplies. War was averted when the Russians, responding to a Western embargo on exports from the Eastern Bloc, lifted the blockade on May 4, 1949.

■ One of the most poignant scenes in the history of baseball, **Babe Ruth** *(top)*, who was dying of cancer, leaning on a bat in his old Yankee uniform on June 13, 1948 during a ceremony celebrating the 25th anniversary of Yankee Stadium, "The House That Ruth Built." Thousands turned out to cheer Ruth a final time; two months later he was dead at 53. This photograph won a Pulitzer Prize for *New York Herald Tribune* photographer Nat Fein. Born in Baltimore in 1895 and raised in an orphanage there, Ruth reached the big leagues as a pitcher with the Boston Red Sox in 1915. An outstanding lefthander, he compiled a 94-46 record before inevitably turning to the outfield because of his hitting ability. In 1920, striking one of the worst bargains in baseball history, Boston sold Ruth to the Yankees for $125,000. As a power-hitting right fielder with New York, Ruth transformed the record book. He led the American League in home runs for 12 years, hitting 60 in 1927 and reaching a total of 714, surpassed only by Hank Aaron in 1974. He joined Lou Gehrig and the other Yankee greats to form the famed "Murderers' Row," dominating the game with a string of World Series victories through the 1920s and early 1930s. In 41 World Series games, Ruth batted .326 with 15 home runs and set a slugging average record which still stands at .744. His colorful, irresponsible, flamboyant personality made Ruth a legend of the period in baseball history he dominated so completely. In 1936 he became one of the first five players elected to the Hall of Fame.

■ Singer **Frank Sinatra** *(middle, left)* in a 1950 photograph. Born in Hoboken, New Jersey in 1915, Sinatra made his recording debut with the Harry James Band in 1939 singing "From the Bottom of My Heart." He went on to become one of the legends of American show business, beginning with his appearances before crowds of screaming fans at New York's Paramount Theatre in the 1940s. This photograph was taken just a few years before Sinatra energized his film-acting career with the performance in *From Here To Eternity* which won him an Oscar as Best Supporting Actor in 1953. Later memorable film roles include *The Man With the Golden Arm* (1955), *The Manchurian Candidate* (1962), and *Von Ryan's Express* (1965).

■ **Norman Rockwell** *(middle, right)*, America's favorite twentieth-century illustrator, whose humorous and subtly incisive pictures of American life looked back toward a simpler age of traditional homespun values. Rockwell's first cover for the *Saturday Evening Post* was published in 1916. He went on to draw 321 more *Post* covers which appeared regularly until 1963. Rockwell died in 1978 at the age of 84.

Five years after the end of World War II, the Cold War between the United States and the Soviet Union and their respective allies erupted into a shooting war in Korea, which dragged on inconclusively for three years and cost approximately five million people their lives—including over 33,000 American soldiers. Political maneuvering between the major powers at the end of World War II left the Korean peninsula divided uneasily along the 38th parallel with a communist country in the north, the Democratic People's Republic of Korea, and in the south, the Republic of Korea, allied with the United States. With Soviet backing, the North Koreans attacked across the 38th parallel on June 25, 1950. Without asking Congress for a declaration of war, President Truman immediately ordered U.S. forces into action in support of the United Nations' "police action" to halt the North Koreans. The early fighting went badly for the United States: the four U.S. divisions which were rushed into action were driven back to the area around Pusan in the southeast. This photograph, taken in early September, 1950, shows **an exhausted American GI** *(top)* taking a break from heavy fighting on the Taegu front.

On September 15, 1950, the Korean tide began to turn as U.N. troops commanded by Douglas MacArthur made a major amphibious landing at Inchon, the port of Seoul, about 100 miles below the 38th parallel. The North Korean lines were cut, and by the end of the month the U.N. forces were totally in control of South Korea. Ignoring Chinese warnings, the U.N. forces then invaded North Korea with the declared intention of reuniting the country. This plan backfired as a huge Chinese army entered the conflict on the side of the North Koreans, and by the middle of December, 1950, the U.N. forces had been driven back to the 38th parallel. On the last day of the year the Communists attempted another invasion of South Korea, but were unable to make substantial gains; U.N. forces retreated but lines were eventually stabilized at approximately the 38th parallel once more. This photograph, taken a few days after the Inchon landing, shows **an American marine with North Korean prisoners** *(middle)* in front of a tank brought ashore during the landing.

Korea played a major role in American politics in the early 1950s. Truman unquestionably cost the Democratic Party some support when he relieved the venerated MacArthur as U.N. commander in April, 1951 because of differences over whether to bomb Chinese bases—Truman was opposed because he felt it would bring the Soviets into the war. Truce talks began on July 10, 1951, but dragged on indecisively until after the 1952 Presidential election. This photograph, taken on December 7, 1952, shows President-elect **Dwight D. Eisenhower visiting with troops** *(bottom)* of the 3rd Division. Eisenhower had criticized the unpopular war during his campaign and was keeping a promise by visiting Korea immediately after his election. After some sporadic final fighting, an armistice was concluded at Panmunjom on July 27, 1953, leaving Korea physically devastated and as politically divided as the country had been before the fighting started in 1950.

■ **President Harry S. Truman** *(opposite, bottom)* holding a copy of the *Chicago Tribune* for November 4, 1948 erroneously reporting his defeat by New York's Governor Thomas E. Dewey in the previous day's Presidential election. After early returns showed Dewey running ahead, Truman won with a margin of more than two million popular votes. This photograph by Frank Cancellare of the United Press was taken in St. Louis as Truman greeted a crowd of supporters from the train he was taking back to Washington from Kansas City. A Democratic Senator from Missouri, first elected in 1934, Truman was not widely known nationally when chosen to run for Vice President with Roosevelt in 1944. With FDR's sudden death in 1945, it fell to Truman to see World War II to its end—including the fateful decision to use the atomic bomb against Japan—and to conduct the first years of the Cold War while assisting the economic reconstruction of Europe. Dewey was favored when the 1948 campaign began, but Truman's vigorous record, reputation for common sense, and unassailable integrity were enough to bring about his decisive reelection. His second term was dominated by the conflict in Korea and the continuing Cold War in international politics. Truman retired to Independence, Missouri in 1953, wrote his memoirs, and died in 1972.

■ **Maureen Catherine "Little Mo" Connolly** *(left),* shown here at the age of 17 in a 1952 Wightman Cup match in London the year before she became the first woman to win the grand slam of tennis with victories in the 1953 British, American, Australian and French singles championships. Connolly's brilliant playing career—she won three consecutive U.S. singles championships, 1951–53 and three consecutive British singles titles, 1952–54—was cut short by a severe leg injury she received in a horseback riding accident in 1954. A member of the National Lawn Tennis Hall of Fame, she died of cancer in 1968.

■ **Yul Brynner and Gertrude Lawrence** *(left)* perform the classic "Shall We Dance" number from the original production of the musical **The King and I**. Created by composer Richard Rodgers and librettist Oscar Hammerstein II, the team who had produced *Oklahoma!* in 1943. The *King and I* opened at New York's St. James Theatre on March 29, 1951 and ran for 1,246 performances. Based on the novel *Anna and the King of Siam* by Margaret Landon, *The King and I* was the exotic Brynner's greatest vehicle. Counting many revivals in the years following the original production, he played the role on stage more than 4,000 times. "Getting to Know You," and "Hello, Young Lovers" were two other Rodgers and Hammerstein standards from *The King and I*.

■ Television had only begun its transformation of the American entertainment landscape when *I Love Lucy,* starring comedienne **Lucille Ball** *(above)* and her husband Desi Arnaz, made its debut in 1951. The long-running show was an instant success and helped make the half-hour situation comedy an entertainment staple for millions and millions of viewers. Television's beloved Lucy, shown here in a 1952 episode, was a major force in the medium for decades, both in front of the camera, and later through the tremendous success of her production company. She died in 1989.

■ A scene from the Cold War in the American desert, troops of the 11th Airborne Division on maneuvers watching the **testing of an atomic weapon** *(top)* near Las Vegas, Nevada in 1951. In 1957 the United States began testing nuclear weapons underground.

■ The Cold War had its greatest echo on the domestic political front in the meteoric rise and fall of Wisconsin Senator **Joseph R. McCarthy** *(bottom),* who led his anti-Communist witch-hunt from his position as Chairman of the Senate's Government Operations Committee and its permanent subcommittee on investigations. McCarthy and subcommittee counsel Roy M. Cohn are shown here during the Army/McCarthy hearings in 1954. The nationally televised hearings, which went on for 36 days and an unprecedented 197 hours of broadcasting, and attracted a huge audience, were sparked by McCarthy's charge of Communist subversion among Army officers and civilian military officials. The hearings became a debacle for McCarthy when he was exposed to a national audience as a demagogue by opposing counsel Joseph Welch. A few months later, McCarthy had to give up his subcommittee chairmanship when the Republicans lost control of the Senate in the 1954 mid-term elections. On December 2, 1954, he was officially censured by his Senate colleagues for conduct "contrary to Senate traditions." McCarthy, who had been elected to the Senate from Wisconsin in 1946 and reelected in 1952, and who first gained influence on the strength of unproved but often repeated charges of Communist influence in the State Department, never regained his former power and died in 1957. His name entered the American political lexicon as a synonym for debate by innuendo and unproved character assassination.

■ **Rocky Marciano** *(top left)*, the only heavyweight champion to retire undefeated, winner of all 49 of his professional fights. Born Rocco Francis Marchegiano in Brockton, Massachusetts in 1923, Marciano won the heavyweight championship in Philadelphia on September 23, 1952 when he knocked out Jersey Joe Walcott in the 13th round. He defended his championship six times before retiring in 1955; two of his other victims were former champions Ezzard Charles and Joe Louis. Marciano was killed in an airplane crash near Newton, Iowa on August 31, 1969.

■ Two twentieth-century American masters, **Frank Lloyd Wright and Carl Sandburg** *(top center)*, photographed after they appeared on the television program *Omnibus* with Alistair Cooke in 1957. Wright (1867–1959), America's greatest modern architect, established his own practice in 1893. His "Prairie School" architecture became the most important influence on modern residential design in this century. Among his many memorable buildings are a private home, Fallingwater, in Mill Run, Pennsylvania (1936), and New York's Solomon R. Guggenheim Museum (1943–59). Sandburg (1878–1967) came to prominence as poet of the "Chicago Renaissance" at the time of World War I. In his popular books, *Chicago Poems* (1916), *Smoke and Steel* (1920), and *The People, Yes* (1936), he celebrated the lives of America's workers and common people. He also collected, performed and published American folk music, won a Pulitzer Prize in history for his massive Lincoln biography, and wrote several books for children and a lengthy novel based on his interpretation of the American experience, *Remembrance Rock* (1948).

■ Mississippi-born **Elvis Presley** *(top right)* in a photograph taken in 1956, the year he burst onto the popular music scene with such hits as "Heartbreak Hotel," "Don't Be Cruel," and "Blue Suede Shoes." Millions of American teenagers followed his rise—helped by record-setting performances on TV's *Ed Sullivan Show*—and a brief period of Army service in the late 1950s did nothing to erode his popularity. Unlike many pop idols, Presley was able to maintain his position at the top until he died of a drug overdose in 1977 at his Memphis mansion, Graceland, at the age of 42.

■ No one epitomized the early years of the Boston Celtics' dynasty in professional basketball more than guard **Bob Cousy** *(left, middle)*, shown here in a 1957 playoff game against St. Louis. The Celtics went on to win the game, the series, and the first of their championships that year as Cousy was named the League's Most Valuable Player. Following a loss to St. Louis in the finals the following year, Boston won eight consecutive championships between 1959 and 1966 under the leadership of Coach Red Auerbach and Center Bill Russell. Cousy retired from the Celtics after the 1963 season.

■ Comedian **Jack Benny** *(left, bottom)*, whose self-deprecating humor—often centering around insults to his violin playing ability, or lack thereof—brought him to the top of the television world in the 1950s, after decades in which he had dominated comedy on radio, is shown here in 1956 when he appeared at a charity function as a violin soloist with the New York Philharmonic at Carnegie Hall.

■ A 1958 photograph of jazz great **Duke Ellington** *(top left),* composer, pianist, and orchestra leader. Ellington came to prominence in the 1920s when at Harlem's famed Cotton Club he established the band which would make his music famous around the world. Many first-rate jazz artists such as Harry Carney and Johnny Hodges, who started with Ellington in the 1920s, were still with him in the 1960s. After composing and recording such jazz classics as "Mood Indigo," "Blue Serge," and "Bojangles," Ellington turned to new worlds, composing major concert works such as *Black, Brown and Beige* (1943), music for films including Otto Preminger's *Anatomy Of A Murder,* and religious jazz works such as *In the Beginning God,* first performed in 1966. Ellington died in 1974.

■ **Dr. Jonas Salk** *(top center)* of the University of Pittsburgh at about the time American children began receiving widespread inoculation with the polio vaccines that bear his name and which were licensed by the federal government on April 12, 1954. Salk had already tested his vaccines—there were three, as virologists had discovered that polio could be caused by three separate viruses—on 400,000 children, including three of his own. The Salk vaccines were made from dead virus strains. The Sabin vaccine, made from live virus strains, was introduced in 1960. Following the general distribution of these vaccines, paralytic polio, once the most feared childhood disease, was eradicated as an American health problem.

■ Mississippi-born author **William Faulkner** *(top right),* winner of the 1949 Nobel Prize for Literature, is shown here at his writing table in a 1955 photograph. From his first novel *Soldiers' Pay* in 1926 to his last, *The Reivers,* published just before his death in 1962, Faulkner created an immense body of work, mostly chronicling the lives and destinies of the inhabitants of his mythical Yoknapatawpha County. His major works include *The Sound and the Fury, As I Lay Dying, Intruder In the Dust, The Hamlet, The Town,* and *The Mansion.*

■ **Marilyn Monroe** *(right),* the quintessential Hollywood sex symbol of the 1950s, is seen here outside her New York apartment shortly before her June, 1956 marriage to playwright Arthur Miller. After starring in such hits as *Bus Stop, Some Like It Hot,* and *Let's Make Love,* Monroe made her last film, *The Misfits,* with Clark Gable—also his last role—in 1960. Perhaps a suicide, she died in Hollywood in 1962 at the age of 36.

■ A scene from the civil rights struggles of the 1950s as the work continued throughout the South of implementing the Supreme Court's 1954 decision that school segregation was unconstitutional. **Nine black students** *(left top)* at the Little Rock, Arkansas Central High School are shown here leaving school on October 9, 1957 under the protection of a detachment of Arkansas National Guardsmen ordered into the service of the federal government by President Eisenhower. Following attempts by Arkansas Governor Orval Faubus to block the court-approved integration plan, the black students had finally taken their places on September 25, backed by 1,000 paratroopers and 10,000 Guardsmen, pressed into service because of threats of mob violence.

■ The 1960s saw continual confrontation in the South over civil rights for blacks, in many cases over the actual implementing at the grass-roots level of rights which blacks had won in the courts. In this photograph, **civil rights protest marchers** *(left, middle)* are passing a blockade of National Guard bayonets in Memphis, Tennessee on March 29, 1968. Less than a week after this picture was taken, on April 4, 1968, Dr. Martin Luther King, Jr. was murdered in Memphis where he and other activists were helping to organize a strike by the city's sanitation workers.

■ **Three attorneys** *(left, bottom),* George E.C. Hayes, Thurgood Marshall, and James Nabrit, Jr., who argued and won the historic case, *Brown v. Board of Education of Topeka,* before the United States Supreme Court in 1954 in which the Court ruled that segregation in public schools was unconstitutional. This was only one of 32 cases which Marshall argued, winning 29 of them, before the Supreme Court during the years after 1940 when he was chief of the NAACP's legal staff. Marshall was nominated to the U.S. Court of Appeals for the Second Circuit (Connecticut, Vermont, and New York) by President Kennedy in 1961. President Lyndon B. Johnson appointed him U.S. solicitor general in 1965 and nominated him to the Supreme Court in 1967. Marshall, the first black member of the Supreme Court, retired in 1991.

■ **Rosa Parks** *(below)* of Montgomery, Alabama, shown here on December 21, 1956, the day a Supreme Court ruling banning segregation on the city's public transit system went into effect. Parks's arrest December 1, 1955 for refusing to ride at the back of a Montgomery bus had sparked a year-long boycott of the city's buses by blacks led by Reverend Martin Luther King, Jr., then pastor of Montgomery's Dexter Avenue Baptist Church. In December, the city of Montgomery announced that it would comply with the November 13, 1956 Supreme Court ruling declaring segregation on public buses unconstitutional. The case which began with Parks's arrest was an important stage in the battle against segregation in the South, both because of the major legal victory and because the effective boycott by Montgomery's 50,000 blacks provided a compelling demonstration of Dr. King's strategy of nonviolence.

■ New York Yankee Manager **Casey Stengel** *(bottom left)*, talking to reporters at Milwaukee's County Stadium during the 1958 World Series. The Yankees won the Series over the Braves, four games to three, redeeming themselves after the previous year's loss to Milwaukee by the same score. The Yankees had little experience of losing under Stengel, who joined the team in 1949 and promptly added his own reign to sport's longest running dynasty by leading his new team to a record five consecutive World Series victories. Five more pennants and two more Series wins completed Stengel's record with the Yankees by the time he left the team after the 1960 season.

■ **Dr. James Dewey Watson** *(bottom center)*, Professor of Biology at Harvard University, photographed in his laboratory in 1962, the year he shared the Nobel Prize for Physiology or Medicine with Francis Crick and Maurice Wilkins of Great Britain for his work in discovering the molecular structure of deoxyribonucleic acid (DNA), the gene substance which is the basis of heredity. Working at the Cavendish Laboratories of Cambridge University in England in the 1950s, Watson and Crick formulated the famous 'double helix' model of the DNA molecule, showing how the molecule could duplicate itself.

■ **Bob Dylan and Joan Baez** *(bottom right)*, folk singers whose early years as entertainers were rooted in the protest movements of the 1960s, photographed in London in 1965. Dylan's first records, released in the early 1960s, included such songs as "Blowin' in the Wind" and "The Times They Are A-Changin'," which became anthems of the civil rights and anti-war movements. Dylan and Baez often performed at civil rights demonstrations in the 1960s—both sang for the crowd of 200,000 at Washington's Lincoln Memorial on August 28, 1963, the day Dr. Martin Luther King, Jr. gave his "I have a dream" speech.

■ A contemplative portrait of the poet **Robert Frost** *(right, top)*, taken shortly before his death in 1963. Born in San Francisco in 1874, Frost moved with his family to New England after the death of his father in 1885. After leaving Harvard because of illness, Frost worked as a farmer and teacher before moving to England just before the start of the first World War. His first slim books, *A Boy's Will* (1913) and *North of Boston* (1914), were immediately popular in the United States; Frost returned to America in 1915 and was soon established as the poet of rural New England. His easy-to-read but profoundly meaningful poetry, exemplified by such poems as "The Road Not Taken" and "Stopping by Woods on a Snowy Evening," gained Frost an audience enjoyed by few modern poets. Frost won the Pulitzer Prize for poetry four times; the impression he left on his countrymen was enhanced by his speech at the inauguration of President Kennedy in 1961.

■ Senator John F. Kennedy makes a point while Vice President Richard M. Nixon waits his turn, a scene from the fourth and final **Kennedy-Nixon Debate** *(right, middle)*. The series of debates in the 1960 campaign marked the first time that Presidential candidates faced each other on television. The consensus of experts was that Kennedy successfully used the debates to overcome Nixon's early advantage of being better known nationally, and that while both were prepared on the issues and both debated well, Kennedy simply projected a Presidential image more effectively than his rival. The polls had Nixon slightly ahead when the debates began, and slightly behind when they ended. On election day, Kennedy won with a paper-thin margin in popular votes, 34,226,731 to 34,108,157, but a more decisive lead, 303 to 219, in electoral votes. From the 1960 race onwards, television has assumed a greater and greater role in the business of electing the President.

■ **President John Fitzgerald Kennedy and Jacqueline Bouvier Kennedy** *(top),* photographed during a White House ceremony nine days before he was assassinated in Dallas on November 22, 1963. Born in 1917, son of Joseph P. Kennedy, businessman and ambassador to Great Britain from 1937 to 1940, Kennedy served in the Navy during World War II and began his political career with election to the House of Representatives from Massachusetts in 1946. In 1952 Kennedy was elected to the Senate and was reelected six years later. In 1960 he won the Democratic nomination and defeated Richard M. Nixon to become the youngest man and the first Roman Catholic to be elected President. Kennedy's "New Frontier" promised a dynamic approach to dealing with national and international problems; successes included the formation of the Alliance for Progress program to aid Latin America, the establishment of the Peace Corps, and the development of an accelerated space program. The disastrous Bay of Pigs invasion of Cuba in April, 1961, which Kennedy's administration supported, failed to oust Fidel Castro and provoked an increased Russian presence there. Concern over Russian nuclear weapons in Cuba led to a confrontation with the Soviets in 1962 when Kennedy ordered a naval quarantine of the island. Retreating from the nuclear brink, Soviet Premier Khrushchev ordered Russian missiles removed from Cuba. Another victory for Kennedy was the signing of a limited nuclear test-ban treaty by the United States, Russia, and Great Britain in 1963. Many domestic policies still in the planning stage had not been implemented when Kennedy was killed; he was the fourth President to be assassinated and the eighth to die in office. The government commission investigating the assassination, chaired by Chief Justice Earl Warren, ruled that the assassination was the work of a single assassin, Lee Harvey Oswald, a view which has been challenged many times by researchers with conflicting theories.

■ **The hands of President Lyndon B. Johnson** *(left),* signing his historic Civil Rights Act into law on July 3, 1964. The most comprehensive civil rights legislation in American history, the bill—passed after a cloture motion ended a Southern filibuster against it in the Senate—prohibited racial discrimination in public accommodations, unions, employment, and all federally funded programs.

■ **Vice President Lyndon Baines Johnson** *(opposite, middle)* being sworn in as President by U.S. District Judge Sarah T. Hughes on *Air Force One,* the Presidential plane, at the Dallas airport on November 22, 1963, the day John F. Kennedy was assassinated. Beside Johnson are his wife, Lady Bird *(left),* and Jacqueline Kennedy. Born in Texas in 1908, Johnson entered politics in the 1930s as a supporter of Franklin Delano Roosevelt's New Deal. He served in Congress from 1938 to 1948, when he was elected to the Senate, with time out for duty in the Navy during World War II. In 1953 he became the Democratic leader in the Senate. A master parliamentarian, Johnson wielded great power in the Senate during the 1950s, and surprised many colleagues and friends when he agreed to run for Vice President with Kennedy in 1960. Succeeding to the Presidency when Kennedy was assassinated, Johnson pushed many significant programs through Congress, including Medicare for the elderly, voting-rights and civil rights legislation, and the initiative he described as his "war on poverty." Johnson was elected in his own right in 1964 with a landslide victory over conservative Republican Barry Goldwater of Arizona. The war in Vietnam, initiated before Johnson took office, proved to be his political Achilles heel. With no end of the interminable conflict in sight, Johnson violated campaign promises not to expand the war; as each escalation of the conflict failed to bring its conclusion closer, Johnson was faced with increasingly vocal opposition at home. Recognizing his loss of support because of Vietnam, Johnson announced that he would not seek reelection in 1968, retiring to Texas where he wrote his memoirs. Johnson died in 1973, less than a week before the agreement to end the war in Vietnam was signed.

■ **The Rev. Martin Luther King, Jr.** *(top)* waving to participants at the largest civil-rights demonstration in American history, the August 28, 1963 "March on Washington," when 200,000 protesters assembled at the Lincoln Memorial to urge passage of civil rights legislation, which came the following year. It was on this occasion that King, president of the Southern Christian Leadership Conference, delivered his famous "I have a dream" speech. Born in Atlanta in 1929, King received degrees from Morehouse College, Crozer Theological Seminary, and Boston University. A Baptist minister in Montgomery, Alabama, King led the boycott which forced desegregation of the city's transit system in 1956. During the 1950s and 1960s, King headed the national civil rights movement, stressing the use of nonviolent protest. He won the Nobel Peace Prize in 1964 and was assassinated on April 4, 1968, at the age of 39, in Memphis, Tennessee, shot at long range while standing on a motel balcony. King's killing sparked rioting in black neighborhoods throughout the country in which at least 45 people were killed. In June, 1968, James Earl Ray was arrested and charged with King's murder; he was sentenced to 99 years in prison.

■ **Black Muslim minister Malcolm X** *(bottom),* addressing a Harlem rally in support of integration efforts in Birmingham, Alabama on May 15, 1963. Six months after this picture was taken, Malcolm X was suspended by Black Muslim leader Elijah Muhammad because of Malcolm X's remarks on the Kennedy assassination, that it was "a case of chickens coming home to roost," i.e. the result of the violence which whites had perpetrated against black Americans for so long. Born Malcolm Little in Omaha, Nebraska in 1925, Malcolm X grew up in Michigan, where his family's house was burned down by the Ku Klux Klan, and where he heard his father, a Baptist minister, endorse the back-to-Africa ideas of Marcus Garvey. He turned to the Black Muslims while serving a prison sentence for burglary from 1946 to 1953, at which time he adopted the name Malcolm X. An eloquent speaker, Malcolm X toured the country on behalf of the Black Muslims, speaking against white political and economic exploitation of blacks. After his break with Elijah Muhammad, Malcolm X formed his own group, the Muslim Mosque, in New York City in 1964. At that time, he reaffirmed his conversion to orthodox Islam, made a pilgrimage to Mecca, and, announcing that he was no longer a racist, entertained the possibility of world brotherhood. Conflicts between Malcolm X's Muslim Mosque and the Black Muslims were not abated, however. Malcolm X's home in Queens was bombed in February, 1965, and just days later, on February 21, 1965, Malcolm X was shot to death in Harlem at a rally of his supporters. Three blacks were convicted of the murder; it was never proved but was widely believed at the time that the Black Muslims were responsible. As an advocate of violence for self-protection, Malcolm X was considered during his lifetime too militant by the mainstream leadership of the civil rights struggle. His widely-read life story, *The Autobiography of Malcolm X,* (1965), has served to keep his ideas on racial injustice current for later generations.

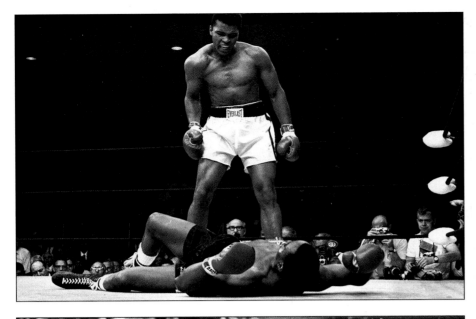

■ **Heavyweight champion Cassius Clay** *(top),* who in 1967 took the Muslim name Muhammad Ali, standing over Sonny Liston after having knocked out the former champion in less than two minutes of the first round of their second fight, at Lewiston, Maine on May 25, 1965. Born in Louisville, Kentucky in 1942, Clay (Ali) had been generally recognized as heavyweight champion after knocking Liston out in the seventh round of their first fight, in Miami on February 25, 1964. After a victory on points over World Boxing Association champion Ernie Terrell in Houston on February 6, 1967, Ali's recognition as champion was unchallenged. In 1967 he refused induction into the armed forces on religious grounds; he was convicted of violating the Selective Service Act, his title was taken from him, and he was barred from boxing. The conviction was reversed by the Supreme Court in 1971. After returning to the ring in 1970, Ali lost a classic 15-round decision to the then heavyweight champion Joe Frazier in New York on March 8, 1971, but regained his title with an 8th-round knockout of George Foreman in Kinshasa, Zaire on October 30, 1974. After several successful defenses, Ali lost the title to Leon Spinks in Las Vegas on February 15, 1978. Defeating Spinks later that year in New Orleans, Ali became thereby the first heavyweight to win the championship three times. He retired in 1979 but later came back to lose two final fights, to Larry Holmes and Trevor Berbick. He is widely regarded today as one of the two or three greatest heavyweights of all time, and a major personality on the world sporting scene during the politically turbulent Vietnam era and its aftermath.

■ **Green Bay Packer fullback Jim Taylor** *(middle)* being tackled by Willie Mitchell of the Kansas City Chiefs in the first quarter of the first Super Bowl at Los Angeles's Memorial Coliseum on January 15, 1967. Johnnie Robinson of the Chiefs (#42) watches the play. Head coach Vince Lombardi's Packers won the game 35-10. Though, as seen here, there were some empty seats—the game was two-thirds sold out—the Super Bowl has since become one of American sport's premier events. The Packers also won the second Super Bowl, their last appearance to date, in Miami on January 14, 1968 with a 33-14 victory over Oakland. The establishment of the Super Bowl as pro football's championship game signified peace between the upstart American Football League, founded in 1960, and the long-established National Football League. By 1970 the leagues were totally merged into one National Football League with American and National Conferences. On January 12, 1969, in the third Super Bowl, the New York Jets, led by quarterback Joe Namath, became the first American Football League team to win the combined championship with a 16 to 7 victory over the Baltimore Colts.

■ **Roberto Clemente, Willie Mays, and Hank Aaron** *(bottom),* three of the National League's star outfielders of the 1950s and 1960s, photographed in San Francisco on July 11, 1961 after all three had been involved in a 10th inning rally to win the All-Star game for the National League by the score of five to four. Clemente played 18 years for Pittsburgh, 1955 to 1972. He led the National League in batting average four times, and compiled a lifetime average of .317. He was the 11th player in history to get 3,000 hits and was the National League's Most Valuable Player in 1966. He died on December 31, 1972 when a cargo plane in which he was flying from Puerto Rico to aid earthquake victims in Nicaragua crashed after takeoff at San Juan International Airport. Clemente was elected to the Hall of Fame in 1973. Mays played 22 seasons in the major leagues, 1951 to 1973, the first 20 and a quarter with the Giants, first in New York, and then in San Francisco after 1957, and the final one and three quarters, comprising 135 games, with the New York Mets. He hit 40 or more home runs six times, and his career total of 660 is third behind Aaron and Babe Ruth; his 1,903 career runs batted in is seventh. Perhaps the greatest defensive outfielder ever to play the game, Mays was the National League's Most Valuable Player in 1954 and 1965; he was elected to the Hall of Fame in 1979. Aaron played 23 seasons in the major leagues, 1954 to 1976, 21 with the Braves, first in Milwaukee and after 1965 in Atlanta, and the final two with the American League's Milwaukee Brewers. The major league career leader in home runs with 755—Aaron surpassed Ruth's 714 in 1974—and in runs batted in with 2,297, Aaron was the National League's Most Valuable Player in 1957 and was elected to the Hall of Fame in 1982.

■ **Senator Robert F. Kennedy** *(left)*
campaigning for the Democratic Presidential nomination in Sacramento, California on May 16, 1968. Three weeks
later, on June 6, Kennedy was shot and
killed in a kitchen corridor of The Ambassador Hotel in Los Angeles after giving his victory speech on winning the
California primary. Kennedy's assassin,
Sirhan Sirhan, apparently acting alone
out of hatred because of Kennedy's
strong support of Israel, was captured
at the scene. Kennedy had served as attorney general in JFK's administration
before being elected to the Senate from
New York in 1964. Lyndon Johnson's decision to step aside in 1968 opened the
way for a stormy battle for the 1968
Democratic Presidential nomination between Senator Eugene McCarthy of
Minnesota, an early opponent of the
Vietnam War, Kennedy, and Vice President Hubert H. Humphrey. After
Kennedy's murder, the Democratic
Convention, held in the Chicago Amphi-
theater in August was marked by passionate debate inside over the Party's
Vietnam policy and by violent confrontation in the streets outside between anti-
war protesters and Chicago's police.
Humphrey won the nomination over Mc-
Carthy, but lost the close election to
Richard M. Nixon by half a million popular votes out of 63 million cast and,
more decisively, by 301 to 191 in electoral votes.

■ **The 101st Airborne Brigade** *(top left)* crossing a river at Ben Khe, South Vietnam in September, 1965. During the Kennedy Administration, between 1961 and 1963, the number of American military advisers in Vietnam rose from 2,000 to 15,000. In 1964, the North Vietnamese attacked American destroyers in the Gulf of Tonkin, and President Johnson responded with air strikes against North Vietnamese torpedo-boat bases, a move approved by Congress, which authorized Johnson to take all necessary steps "to repel any armed attack" against American forces and "to prevent further aggression." By the end of 1965, as the conflict escalated—a pattern which was to be repeated throughout the war's course—the United States had 184,000 combat troops in South Vietnam and air units heavily engaged in flying combat missions.

■ **Picketing at the White House** *(middle)* in April, 1965. As the war in Vietnam escalated, opposition to it at home escalated as well. At this relatively early demonstration, 5,000 marchers assembled at the White House to call for an end to the war.

■ **An American soldier** *(bottom)* resting during a monsoon near Phuc, South Vietnam while another soldier keeps watch in a June, 1967 photograph by United Press International staff photographer Toshio Sakai which won a Pulitzer Prize in feature photography in 1968. When first published, this picture was titled: "Dreams of a Better Life."

■ **An American marine** *(above)* carefully walking along the bed of a stream filled with deadly pongee sticks imbeded there by the Vietcong. The sticks were spears of bamboo or other wood sharp enough to pierce the sole of a combat boot, if stepped on heavily, and often covered with some poisonous substance. This photograph was taken for the United Press by Nguyen Thanh Tai at an unnamed location in South Vietnam in January, 1967. The following year, American troop strength in Vietnam surpassed half a million, partially in response to the January–February Tet offensive, when Vietcong guerrillas attacked Saigon, Hue, and other cities. In May, 1968 the Paris peace talks began; the talks would, however, drag on for over four years as the fighting continued before an agreement would be signed in 1973.

■ **Helicopters of the U.S. First Air Cavalry Division** *(top)* landing at Lai Khe, South Vietnam on June 13, 1972 on a mission to transport troops of the South Vietnamese Second Division to An Loc, a UPI photograph by Jeff Taylor. President Nixon began limited troop withdrawals shortly after taking office in 1969, while protests at home continued at full strength. Although U.S. ground forces were withdrawn from Cambodia in 1970 and barred by Congress in 1971 from being used further in Laos and Cambodia, Nixon responded to a 1972 North Vietnamese thrust by ordering the mining of North Vietnamese ports and continued bombing attacks on North Vietnam in an attempt to force action at the Paris talks.

■ A scene from **the end of the war in Vietnam** *(middle)*, USAF Captain Michael S. Kerr of Sequim, Washington is reunited with his wife and children at Travis AFB, California on March 7, 1973. Kerr had been a prisoner since he was shot down on a reconnaissance mission over North Vietnam on January 16, 1967. The peace agreement ending the longest war in American history was signed in Paris on January 27, 1973, six weeks before this photograph was taken, and just days after Nixon ordered a halt to offensive operations in North Vietnam. Debate over whether every prisoner captured by the North Vietnamese has been released or accounted for continues to the present time.

■ The last American troops left Vietnam in March, 1973. The following year was marked by charges from both sides that the other was violating the peace agreement. Fighting broke out again in 1975 and the Vietcong scored heavily early in the year. This photograph was taken at **Nha Trang, South Vietnam in early April, 1975** *(bottom)* and shows an American punching a man attempting to board an evacuation plane. After this plane left, Nha Trang was overrun by the Vietcong. As U.S. Marine embassy guards and other American civilians were evacuated at the end of April, South Vietnamese forces surrendered to the Vietcong. The long war in Vietnam and neighboring countries in Southeast Asia cost the United States 47,382 battle deaths, and another 10,753 deaths from related causes. It provoked the most intense political division in the United States since the Civil War. Though the thought provided little comfort, the facts seemed to vindicate American military strategists of the World War II era who believed that the one thing the United States must avoid at all costs was a land war in Asia; this land war had been devastatingly costly, nationally enervating, and ultimately unwinable.

■ The *Apollo 11* spacecraft *(top),* which carried astronauts Neil A. Armstrong, Edwin E. "Buzz" Aldrin, Jr., and Michael Collins on their 238,000-mile journey to the moon, is shown here on top of the Saturn 5 rocket used in the historic launch from Pad 39-A at Cape Kennedy, Florida on July 16, 1969, two days after this photograph was taken. The Apollo program was announced by the National Aeronautics and Space Administration in 1961, and the first manned Apollo flight, *Apollo 7,* took place on October 11, 1968. Three additional missions before *Apollo 11* were utilized to perfect the handling of the Lunar Module in space and to practice reaching and exiting the lunar orbit.

■ Astronaut Edwin E. Aldrin, Jr. *(bottom),* photographed on the moon by *Apollo 11* Commander Neil A. Armstrong on July 20, 1969.

Armstrong and the Lunar Module are reflected in Aldrin's visor. While Collins remained aboard the 50-ton *Apollo* spacecraft in lunar orbit, the Lunar module, the "Eagle," piloted by Armstrong, who took over from the automatic control system 300 feet from the surface to find a flat spot to land, touched down at 4:18 P.M., Eastern Daylight Time on June 20, 1969 in the area known as the Sea of Tranquility *(Mare Tranquilitatis).* At 10:56 P.M., Armstrong stepped from the "Eagle" and became the first human to walk on the moon as hundreds of millions of people around the world watched on television and heard him say, "That's one small step for man, one giant leap for mankind." Armstrong and Aldrin remained on the moon for 21 hours and 37 minutes collecting soil and rock samples, setting up scientific instruments, and taking photographs; the moon's low gravity made it relatively easy for them to maneuver in their 185-pound spacesuits. They rejoined the *Apollo 11* spacecraft on July 21 and landed in the Pacific three days later. After landing, the three astronauts spent 18 days in quarantine as a precaution against contamination by lunar microbes. Subsequent Apollo flights continued the exploration of the moon's surface and the deployment of additional instruments for experiments and seismographic measurement. The last Apollo flight, *Apollo 17,* took place in December, 1972.

■ Euphoria about the success of the space program did nothing to end dissent over the war in Southeast Asia. On May 4, 1970, at **Kent State University** *(opposite, left top)* in Kent, Ohio, a protest against the U.S. invasion of Cambodia turned into a tragic episode of senseless violence as a National Guard unit, ordered to the campus by Ohio Governor James Rhodes following a previous confrontation between students and police, attempted to break up a demonstration which Rhodes had banned. When the students refused to disperse, tear gas was fired to which the students responded by throwing rocks. The soldiers, thinking they heard a gunshot, fired on a group of students at a distance of 25 yards. Four student bystanders including one R.O.T.C. member were killed—one of the dead is shown here in a UPI photograph—and ten were wounded.

■ **President Richard M. Nixon** *(opposite, right top)* and Secretary of State William Rogers flanking Chinese Deputy Premier Li Hsien-Nien during a visit to the Great Wall on Nixon's historic February, 1972 trip to the People's Republic of China, establishing direct communication between the U.S. and Communist China after a 21-year break. In May, 1972, Nixon became the first U.S. President to visit the Soviet Union, at which time agreements with the Russians on arms limitation, trade, and joint space ventures were announced. Nixon was reelected in November over Senator George S. McGovern in one of the most one-sided victories in Presidential history; less that two years later, because of the Watergate scandal, he became the only President to resign the office.

■ **Senator Sam J. Ervin of North Carolina** *(opposite, left bottom),* on the right in this photograph, conferring with Senate colleagues Howard Baker of Tennessee *(left)* and Lowell Weicker of Connecticut (next to Baker) and two staff members during the 1973 hearings of the Select Committee on Presidential Campaign Activities, the committee established to investigate the Watergate burglary and its aftermath. On June 17, 1972, five men had been arrested at the Watergate apartment hotel complex in Wash-

ington, D.C., where they had broken into the national headquarters of the Democratic Party. One of those arrested was the security chief of the Republicans' Committee for the Re-election of the President (CREEP), James McCord. The five were convicted on burglary and wiretapping charges, as were G. Gordon Liddy, the Committee's general counsel, and E. Howard Hunt, a former White House aide. When McCord contacted the judge in the case, U.S. District Judge John J. Sirica, and claimed that the White House had urged the seven defendants to plead guilty and remain silent, the grand jury was reconvened to look again into the connection between the Watergate burglars and the President's associates. At that time, Jeb Stuart Magruder, assistant to CREEP's head, former Attorney General John N. Mitchell, changed his testimony and stated that the Watergate break-in had been approved by the Committee, and that he had committed perjury earlier at the instigation of Mitchell and the President's counsel, John W. Dean III. It was at this juncture that the Senate hearings under Ervin's chairmanship began. Under relentless scrutiny, President Nixon accepted responsibility for the actions of his staff, though claiming he had no knowledge of the break-in or the attempts to cover it up, and announced the dismissal of Dean and the resignations of some of his key aides and advisors, including H.R. Haldeman and John D. Erlichman. During the Ervin hearings, a member of the White House staff, Alexander P. Butterfield, revealed what became the crucial fact for the remainder of the time that Watergate occupied the nation's attention—that conversations in the President's office had routinely been secretly recorded. While lengthy legal sparring ensued over attempts to gain access to the tapes, the President's reluctance to release them, and the revelation that some tapes when released had unaccountable gaps, parallel inquiries into the Watergate participants' campaign practices revealed a number of other so-called "dirty tricks" perpetrated during the 1972 campaign. These included using federal agencies to harass the political opponents of the President and employing a secret White House intelligence unit to burglarize the office of the psychiatrist of Daniel Ellsberg, a former Dept. of Defense employee who had released to the news media the classified "Pentagon Papers" on the Vietnam War. Responding to all of these developments, the House Judiciary Committee took up the question of formal impeachment charges against the President, whose fortunes suffered a blow when the Supreme Court ruled that he did not have the authority to withhold tapes of conversations which pertained to criminal cases. Responding to the new tapes, the Judiciary Committee voted to recommend impeachment in late July, 1974, stressing the role which the White House had played in obstructing justice in the Watergate affair. On August 5, 1974, Nixon admitted that he had tried to prevent the FBI from investigating the connection between the Watergate break-in and his staff. As his remaining support in Congress crumbled following that revelation, the President resigned on August 8, 1974.

■ **President Nixon** *(opposite, right bottom)* leaving the White House on August 9, 1974, following his farewell speech to his staff. He was succeeded by Gerald R. Ford who granted Nixon an unconditional pardon on September 8. His three most powerful advisers, Mitchell, Haldeman, and Erlichman, along with a host of others, all were sentenced to prison terms for their roles in Watergate.

■ **Betty Friedan** *(right),* a
pivotal figure in the feminist
movement of the 1960s and
1970s, whose seminal book
The Feminine Mystique
(1963) examined the frustra-
tion and dissatisfaction felt
by women confined by society to traditional roles. In
1966 Friedan helped found
the National Organization for
Women, of which she was
the first president. This 1983
photograph was taken at a
Washington, D.C. banquet
marking the 20th anniver-
sary of *The Feminine
Mystique.*

■ **The American Ice Hockey team** *(below)* celebrating their momentous victory over the Russians, four goals to three, on February 22, 1980 during the winter Olympic Games at Lake Placid, New York. While most of the team is piling on the American goalie, Jim Craig, Neal Broten (#9) and Dave Silk (#8) flank John O'Callahan, who has Mike Ramsey pinned to the ice. The U.S. team went on to win the hockey gold medal for the first time since 1960. The four Olympic hockey gold medals between 1960 and 1980 had all been won by the Russians.

■ **Mary Lou Retton** *(right, top)* on the balance beam during the 1984 Olympic Games in Los Angeles. Her stunning victory in women's gymnastics led the American team to new heights in a field which only a few years before had been the exclusive preserve of teams from Russia and Eastern Europe, and marked the coming of age of the sport of gymnastics in America.

■ Part of the crowd of 50,000 New Yorkers **holding a silent vigil** *(right, middle)* on December 14, 1980 in New York's Central Park to mourn the murder of former Beatle John Lennon. Six days before, on December 8, Lennon and his wife Yoko Ono were returning to their home in the Dakota apartments at 72nd Street and Central Park West when Lennon was shot four times and killed by a deranged fan and sometime amateur guitarist, David Chapman, who waited at the scene to be arrested reading a copy of J.D. Salinger's *Catcher in the Rye*. A cultural phenomenon of the 1960s was the invasion of the American popular music scene by British groups and singers. On their arrival in New York in February, 1964 for their first American tour, the Beatles were greeted with wild enthusiasm by their legions of teen-aged American fans, and a record 73 million watched them perform on the Ed Sullivan TV show. Many of their countrymen, The Rolling Stones, The Who, Elton John and others, gave the memorable music of the 1960s a decidedly British flavor.

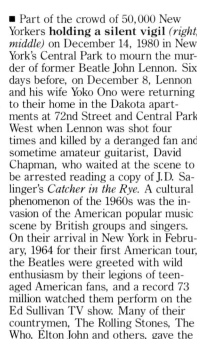

■ **The Vietnam Veterans Memorial** *(above),* designed by Yale University architecture student Maya Yang Lin, was dedicated at a tree-shaded area near the Lincoln Memorial in Washington, D.C. on November 13, 1982. The names of more than 58,000 Americans who died as a result of the Vietnam War are inscribed on the Memorial's polished black granite surface.

■ **An AIDS Candlelight March** *(opposite, right bottom)* in New York City on May 2, 1983. From mid-1981, when AIDS was first reported in the United States, to the present, when there have been over 190,000 reported cases—and over 125,000 deaths—the disease went from being totally unknown to being one of the nation's, and the world's, greatest health threats. A defect in the body's natural immunity to disease caused by a virus, the human immunodeficiency virus or HIV, AIDS is spread through sexual contact, sharing of needles by intravenous drug users, and less often through transfused blood. With no cure in sight, the World Health Organization has predicted that there may be five to six million new cases of AIDS worldwide by the year 2000.

■ **Singer Bruce Springsteen** *(right),* photographed here performing his 1984 hit "Born in the U.S.A." in Washington, D.C. at the start of a 1985 U.S. tour. Springsteen's hard-edged but often melancholy rock music evoked echoes of the turmoil of an America passing through the troubled times of the Vietnam era and its aftermath.

■ **President Jimmy Carter** *(below)* flanked by Israeli Prime Minister Menachem Begin and Egyptian President Anwar el-Sadat. After Carter won a close election in 1976 over incumbent Gerald R. Ford, his one term in office was beset by many problems—the energy crisis, high inflation and interest rates, and the inability to free the hostages taken at the United States Embassy in Teheran, Iran on November 4, 1979. Carter enjoyed a bright moment in the international sphere in September, 1978 when he successfully brought Begin and Sadat together for a thirteen-day conference at Camp David resulting in agreement on a "framework for peace," which was followed up by the signing of a formal peace treaty between Israel and Egypt at the White House on March 26, 1979. Begin and Sadat shared the 1978 Nobel Peace Prize for their efforts. Though no other Arab countries took part, the peace between Israel and Egypt which Carter worked so hard to bring about has proved to be a lasting one. Ironically, in 1981 Sadat was assassinated in Egypt while reviewing a military parade commemorating the Arab-Israeli war of October, 1973.

■ **President Ronald Reagan and Mikhail S. Gorbachev** *(left)* on November 21, 1985 at their Geneva summit meeting. Gorbachev, as Secretary General of Russia's Communist Party, became the political leader of the Soviet Union in 1985 following the death of Konstantin U. Chernenko. Reagan, born in Tampico, Illinois in 1911, worked as a radio sports announcer in Des Moines, Iowa in the middle 1930s. After arriving in Hollywood later in the decade, he spent about 30 years as a successful film and television actor—and served as president of the Screen Actors Guild during part of the anti-communist hysteria of the post-World War II period—gradually becoming more conservative in his political orientation. After years as a television spokesman for the General Electric Company, a period which helped him sharpen his already impressive oratorical ability, Reagan won the California Governorship in 1966 over Edmund G. Brown on a platform calling for spending cuts. Elected President in 1980 by a wide majority—489 electoral votes to 49 for Carter—Reagan introduced the American economy to "supply-side" economics, attempting to stimulate production while controlling inflation by cutting taxes and curtailing government spending. After a recession during the early years of his administration, Reagan's fortunes improved as the economy entered a sustained period of growth and moderate inflation, but which had a dark side in the huge federal budget deficits Reagan was unable to control, and for which many blamed his policies as freely as he blamed those of his opponents. Reagan survived an assassination attempt early in his presidency, and, later in his tenure, a major political scandal involving the sale of arms to a hostile Iran for money which was illegally diverted to the Nicaraguan Contras by his aides. It was a feature of his Presidency often marveled at by his detractors that little of the criticism the government earned under his leadership ever "stuck" to Reagan personally, so great was his popularity with the majority of the electorate. On the international front, Reagan scored several victories. The hostages in Iran were freed on the day he took office, terrorism in the Middle East was countered somewhat more effectively than by previous administrations, and relations with the Soviet Union improved, exemplified by Reagan's personal relationship with Gorbachev, which was warm enough to keep them talking through the 1985 summit despite differences over Russia's record on human rights and Reagan's interest in the "Star Wars" space defense program. After the successful 1985 summit, superpower relations faltered when a 1986 meeting between Reagan and Gorbachev in Reykjavik, Iceland broke up suddenly over the President's refusal to abandon Star Wars. Back on track in 1987, Reagan and Gorbachev met in Washington, and on December 8 finally signed a comprehensive arms control treaty which included procedures for verification inspections to insure compliance by both sides, a major stumbling block for years. Reagan visited Russia in 1986 as his second term was ending; later that year Gorbachev, speaking to the United Nations, declared that the Cold War was over.

■ **Cincinnati Red Pete Rose,** *(top right),* photographed in 1985, the year he capped his 23-year playing career by surpassing Ty Cobb's record, in the books since 1928, of 4,191 lifetime hits. Rose hit a single off San Diego's Eric Show on September 11, 1985 to replace Cobb in the record books; he finished his playing career with 4,256 hits and no imminent challengers on the horizon. The euphoria many of Rose's fans felt on his shattering of one of baseball's "untouchable" records was tempered in recent years by Rose's banishment from baseball for gambling and his imprisonment in 1990 on income-tax evasion charges. Still at issue is the question of whether Rose's on-field accomplishments will be enough to gain his eventual admission to the Hall of Fame.

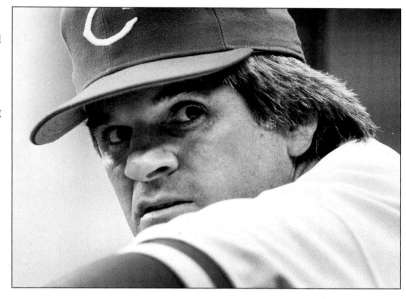

■ Part of the crowd at Cape Canaveral, Florida on January 28, 1986 witnessing the **explosion of the Space Shuttle Challenger** *(bottom right),* the worst disaster in the history of America's space program. The *Challenger* exploded 73 seconds after liftoff, while traveling 2,900 feet per second at a height of nine miles; thousands of pieces of debris were scattered over a wide area. All seven astronauts were killed—Commander Francis "Dick" Scobee, Commander Michael J. Smith, Dr. Judith A. Resnik, Dr. Ronald E. McNair, Lieutenant Colonel Ellison S. Onizuka, Gregory B. Jarvis, and Christa McAuliffe, a New Hampshire schoolteacher who had become a popular hero after she was selected and rigorously trained for the *Challenger's* mission. A panel authorized by President Reagan to investigate the causes of the tragedy placed the blame on a defective seal on a solid fuel booster rocket. The space program went through a period of reexamination following the *Challenger* disaster; on September 29, 1988 the shuttle *Discovery* lifted off from Cape Canaveral on a mission to launch a $100 million communication satellite, putting the space program back in operation.

■ America has always been justly described as a nation of immigrants, a process which began at the start of our history and continues today, as illustrated by this photograph taken at Miami's Orange Bowl on September 17, 1984, when almost 10,000 people became **naturalized American citizens** *(below),* the largest such event in the nation's history. The records of the Immigration and Naturalization Service of the Department of Justice show that between 1820 and 1989, 54,978,717 people were immigrants to America, including almost ten million from Great Britain and Ireland combined, and just over seven million from Germany, more than from any other single country. No part of the world is unrepresented in these records, an enduring fact of our nation's rich and varied heritage.

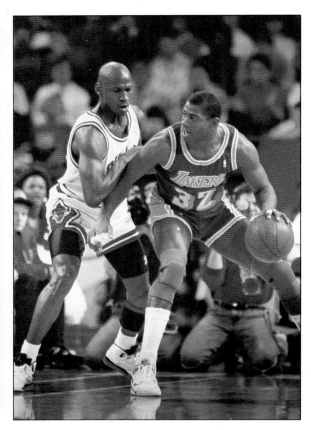

■ The blond of the 1980s, **singer-actress Madonna** *(above left)*, shown here at the 1991 Academy Awards presentations performing the Oscar-nominated song "Sooner or Later" from the movie *Dick Tracy,* in which she appeared with Warren Beatty.

■ **Composer-conductor Leonard Bernstein** *(above center),* leading an orchestra at the East Berlin Schauspielhaus on December 23, 1989, not long before his death. Born in 1918, Bernstein came to prominence in the 1940s in appearances with the New York Philharmonic, where he was Bruno Walter's assistant conductor, and the City Center orchestras. In 1958, he became the New York Philharmonic's permanent conductor, and during the following decade was a vigorous force in the musical world, conducting international tours, appearing with his orchestra as a piano soloist, and making memorable television appearances which served to popularize classical music. Bernstein retired as a full-time conductor in 1969. As a composer, he made his mark in various idioms with classical works including his oratorio *Kaddish* (1963), a composition which makes use of Jewish liturgical themes, his *Mass,* composed for the opening of the John F. Kennedy Center for the Performing Arts in Washington, D.C. in 1971, ballets such as *Fancy Free* (1944), and musical comedies including *On the Town* (1944), *Candide* (1956), and the spectacularly popular *West Side Story* (1957).

■ State-of-the-art basketball as showcased during the 1990–1991 season by Los Angeles Laker **Earvin "Magic" Johnson** *(above right),* with the ball, being guarded here by the Chicago Bulls' Michael Jordan. Johnson's Lakers won four NBA titles in the 1980s; the Bulls finished on top in 1991. In the fall of 1991, Johnson shocked the sports world by announcing his retirement due to infection by the HIV virus.

■ **President George Bush and Russian President-elect Boris Yeltsin** *(right)* at the White House on June 20, 1991. Elected America's 41st President in 1988 after serving two terms as Vice President under Ronald Reagan, Bush has earned high marks with the electorate for his overall handling of foreign affairs, including the continuing thaw in American-Soviet relations which began in the Reagan era. Bush's "approval rating" soared in the winter of 1991 as Operation Desert Storm, the nation's largest military enterprise since World War II, forced Iraq's Saddam Hussein to remove his forces from Kuwait, which the Iraqis had invaded and occupied in August, 1990. On the domestic front, Bush has drawn criticism for ineffective leadership in the face of a faltering economy and a serious recession, the multi-billion dollar cost to the taxpayer of repaying losses incurred during recent Republican administrations by failed Savings and Loan institutions, and inability to address serious national concerns such as the spiraling cost of health care, and federal budget deficits which appear to continue out of control despite the tax policy changes of the Reagan years.

■ **Lance Corporal John Clark**
(right, top) of the 3rd Battalion, 6th
Marines, practicing firing a mortar
with his unit in Saudi Arabia in January, 1991, as Operation Desert Storm
was under way. Actual timing of the
transition from the defensive Operation Desert Shield to the offensive Operation Desert Storm was placed in
the hands of the military on the scene
when the January 15 deadline was
passed without Iraqi action to vacate
Kuwait. The decision to start the war
on January 16, 1991 was made by the
American commander in the Gulf,
General H. Norman Schwarzkopf.

■ **Soldiers of the 82nd Airborne
Division** *(below)* exiting from a C-5A
transport plane at an air base in Saudi
Arabia in August, 1990, shortly after
the beginning of Operation Desert
Shield. Iraq had annexed neighboring
Kuwait early in August, 1990. An
American military build-up, Operation
Desert Shield, immediately began in
the Gulf, as political and economic
sanctions were applied to Iraq in an attempt to isolate the Saddam Hussein
regime and force them to leave
Kuwait. Sanctions having failed, President Bush obtained, after a historic
debate, Congressional approval to take
military action to force Iraq out of
Kuwait; toward the end of 1990, January 15, 1991 was established as a final
deadline before which the shooting
war would not start.

■ **U.S. Marines** *(right, middle)* from
the 3rd Battalion, 7th Marines playing
volleyball in the desert of Saudi Arabia
as a CH-53 transport helicopter takes
off behind them. This photograph was
taken on November 9, 1990. U.S.
troop strength in the Gulf was
540,000 at the height of the war. The
U.S. and allies flew over 116,000 air
sorties during Operation Desert
Storm, losing 57 aircraft and helicopters. The allied strategy was to pound
Iraq from the air for the first weeks of
the war; a brief ground assault in late
February brought the liberation of
Kuwait, which was left physically devastated by bomb damage and fires
deliberately set by Iraq throughout
the oil fields.

■ **Kimberly Cano** *(right, bottom)* of
the Aviation Regiment of the U.S.
Army's 18th Airborne photographed
here at a Saudi air base in September,
1990, shortly after her unit had arrived following a 20-hour flight from
Fort Bragg, North Carolina. A feature
of Operations Desert Shield and Desert Storm was the appearance of female soldiers closer to combat than
ever before in U.S. history. Six per
cent of the 540,000 U.S. troops deployed in the Gulf were women. Three
hundred and twenty-two U.S. troops,
including eight women, were killed in
the Gulf, 136 of them in combat. The
number of Iraqi soldiers killed cannot
be determined with precision, but is
estimated at between 50,000 and
100,000.

■ The American commander in the Gulf, **General H. Norman Schwarzkopf** *(below)*, photographed on parade in Washington, D.C. on June 8, 1991.

■ New York gave Persian Gulf veterans the city's traditional welcome home with this **ticker-tape parade up Broadway** *(far left)* on June 10, 1991. The end of Operation Desert Storm was greeted with relief that American and allied casualties had been so light, but with some disappointment at the inability of the allied forces to cause the overthrow of Saddam Hussein's regime despite the devastation of both his military machine and Iraq's infrastructure.

■ **Judge Clarence Thomas** *(right)*, of the United States Court of Appeals taking the oath prior to testifying before the Senate Judiciary Committee on October 11, 1991. Nominated by President George Bush in the summer of 1991 to replace the recently retired Justice Thurgood Marshall, and thereby become the Supreme Court's 106th member, Thomas had earlier testified at length before the Judiciary Committee as a routine part of the Senate confirmation process. His critics, primarily Democrats, complained during and after Thomas's original Judiciary Committee appearances that he had not revealed his positions on crucial public questions, including abortion rights and the possibility that the Court might modify or overturn the landmark abortion decision, *Roe v. Wade*. Because he had not made clear his position on civil rights and was viewed as a conservative Republican, many traditional Civil Rights organizations also remained hostile to the nomination of Thomas. With the Judiciary Committee split on the question of Thomas's qualifications for the Court, the nomination went to the full Senate for a decision. Shortly before the confirmation vote was to be held,

it became public knowledge, through confidential documents leaked to the press by opponents of the Thomas nomination, that University of Oklahoma Law Professor Anita Hill, who had worked for Thomas in the 1980s at the Department of Education's office for civil rights, and later at the Equal Employment Opportunity Commission, where he had been Chairman, had made allegations, which she had not intended to make public, of sexual harassment against Thomas to investigators for the Judiciary Committee. The charges had, before they became public, been investigated for the Committee by the Federal Bureau of Investigation, which had been unable to confirm or refute them. The Judiciary Committee went back into session to debate the harassment charges and held the American people prisoner to their television screens during the weekend of October 11–13 while a parade of witnesses followed the two protagonists of the drama and testified for and against Hill and Thomas. While Hill impressed many viewers as a credible witness, Thomas resolutely denied her allegations without qualification. After lengthy debate, the Committee remained split along

mostly partisan lines with Republicans trying to discredit Hill and continuing to back the nomination of Thomas and Democrats adding belief in Hill's testimony to their earlier view that Thomas, who had served as a Federal judge only for a short time, was hardly the best qualified person in America for the vacant Supreme Court position. With the nation paying unprecedented attention to a confirmation vote, the full Senate debated the matter on October 15 and ended by confirming the Thomas nomination to the Supreme Court by the narrow vote of 52–48. The episode aroused controversy over the fairness of the nomination/confirmation process and questions in the minds of many over the ability of Congress to fulfill effectively the "advise and consent" role outlined for it by the Constitution. More than this, the Judiciary Committee's hearings on the sexual harassment charges specifically focused national attention on that issue more effectively than anything had done up to that time, symbolizing the changes in attitudes which had been occurring since the start of the feminist movement in the 1960s.

Picture Index

All pictures are indexed by the name of each person represented or, in some cases, the event pictured. Following the page number in each entry is a source code (in parenthesis) and, when available, the name of the artist or photographer (in italics).

Aaron, Hank, 118(B)
Adams, John, 22(A) *Gilbert Stuart*
AIDS Candlelight march, 124(A) *Rich Wandel*
Alamo, 29(A)
Alaska Gold Rush, 59(A)
Alaska, Purchase of, 42(A)
Alcott, Louisa May, 42(A)
Aldrin, Edwin E. Jr., "Buzz," 122(B)
American and French troops, WWI, 77(A)
American bombers, WWII, France, 101(B)
American bombers, WWII, Pacific, 101(B)
American troops, France, 76(A)
American troops on the Western Front, WWI, 76(A)
Anderson, Marian, 83(A)
Anthony, Susan B., 62(A)
Anti-Vietnam War demonstration, 120(B)
Apollo 11, 122(B)
Armistice Day, 1918, 78(A)
Armstrong, Louis, 106(A)
Astaire, Fred and Ginger Rogers, 91(B)
Audubon, John James, 29(A)
Ayres, Agnes, 84(B)

Baez, Joan, 115(B)
Baker, Howard, 123(B)
Ball, Lucille, 110(B)
Bardeen, Dr. John, 107(B)
Barrow, Clyde and Bonnie Parker, 91(B)
Baseball, game in 1887, 52(A) *Pruny*
Begin, Menachem, 126(B) *Tim Murphy*
Bell, Alexander Graham, 47(A)
Benny, Jack, 112(B)
Berlin, Irving, 79(A)
Berlin Airlift, 107(A)
Bernstein, Leonard, 128(C) *Juergen Schwarz*
Bonhomme Richard vs. *Serapis* 20(E) *James Hamilton*
Boone, Daniel, 13(H) *George Caleb Bingham*
Booth, John Wilkes, 41(B)
Boston Massacre, 14(D) *Paul Revere*
Boston Tea Party, 14(A)
Bradley, Omar, 102(A)
Brady, Mathew, 39(A)
Brattain, Walter H., 107(B)
Brooklyn Bridge, completed, 51(D)
Brooklyn Bridge, workmen on, 51(A)
Brown, John, 33(A)
Bryan, William Jennings, 82(A)
Brynner, Yul, 110(A)
Buffalo Shooting, 50(A)
Bunker Hill, Battle of, 16(A) *John Trumbull*
Burr, Aaron, 24(A)
Bush, George, 128(B) *Joe Marquette*

Cadillac, Antoine Laumet de La Mothe, sieur de, 12(A)
Calamity Jane, 47(A)
California Gold Rush, 31(A)
California Gold Rush, advertisement for passage, 31(A)
Carter, Jimmy, 126(B) *Tim Murphy*
Carver, George Washington, 80(A)
Casablanca, 96(A)
Challenger explodes, 127(B) *Bill Mitchell*
Chaplin, Charlie, 79(B)
Chicago Columbian Exposition, 58(A)
Chicago Fire, 45(B)
Child Laborers, 69(A) *Lewis Hine*
Churchill, Winston, 103(A)
Civil War, casualty, 38(A)
Clark, William, 25(A) *N.C. Wyeth*
Clay, Cassius (Muhammad Ali), 118(B)
Clemente, Roberto, 118(B)
Cobb, Ty, 71(A)
Cody, Buffalo Bill and Sitting Bull, 50(A)
Cohan, George M. and family, 79(B)
Cohn, Roy M., 111(B)
Columbus, Christopher, 2(E) *Edward A. Abbey*
Connolly, Maureen "Little Mo", 110(B)
Constitution, Preamble, 21(A)
Constitution, Signing of, 21(F) *J.B. Stearns*
Constitution v. *Guerrière* 26(A)
Coogan, Jackie, 79(B)
Corliss Engine, 48(A)
Cornwallis's surrender at Yorktown, 20(E) *John Trumbull*
Coronado, Francisco Vásquez de, 3(A)
Cousy, Bob, 112(B)
Cowboys, 50(A) *Frederic Remington*
Crockett, Davy, 29(A)
Curtiss, Biplane, 70(A)
Custer, George Armstrong, 46(A)

Dance marathon couple, 81(A)
Darrow, Clarence, 82(A)
Davis, Jefferson, inauguration, 35(A)
Declaration of Independence, The, 18(E) *John Trumbull*
Dempsey, Jack and Gene Tunney, 84(A)
Depression, Black Tuesday, 88(B)
Depression, breadline, 88(A)
Depression, apple seller, 89(B)
Depression, unemployment line, 89(B)
Dickinson, Emily, 33(A)
Didrikson, Mildred, "Babe," 90(B)
DiMaggio, Joe, 97(B)
Doolittle, Jimmy H., 100(B)
Douglas, Stephen A., 35(A)
Douglass, Frederick, 56(A)
Drake, Sir Francis, 4(A)

Dust storms on the Plains, 92(B)
Dylan, Bob, 115(B)
de León, Juan Ponce, 3(A)
de Soto, Hernando, 3(A)

Earhart, Amelia, 93(A)
Edison, Thomas, 48(A)
Einstein, Albert, 80(A)
Eisenhower, Dwight, 109(B)
Eisenhower, Dwight, 102(A)
Ellington, Duke, 113(B)
Ellis Island, immigrants arriving, 65(B)
Ellis Island, immigrants at lunch, 64(B)
Ellis Island, immigrant woman, 64(A) *Lewis Hine*
Ellis Island, Italian immigrant woman, 64(A) *Lewis Hine*
Ellis Island doctor, 64(A)
Emigrants crossing the plains, 44(A) *Darley and Hall*
Empire State Building, 90(B)
Erie Canal, 28(A) *J.H. Bufford, W. Wilson*
Ervin, Sam, 123(B)
Execution of Lincoln assassination conspirators, 41(A)

Faulkner, William, 113(B)
Flatiron Building, 70(A)
Football, first intercollegiate game, 44(A) *W.N. Boyd*
Ford, Henry, 59(A)
Ford assembly line, 71(A)
Foster, Stephen, 30(A)
Franklin, Benjamin, 24(A) *Charles Willson Peale*
Fredericksburg, battle of, 36(A)
French and Indian War, 13(A) *Rufus Zogbaum*
Friedan, Betty, 123(B)
Frost, Robert, 115(B)
Fur Traders Descending the Missouri, 32(G) *George Caleb Bingham*

G.I.'s celebrate at Nurnberg, 103(B)
Geronimo, 53(A)
Gershwin, George, 80(A)
GI's in Brest, France, 101(B)
Golden Gate Bridge, 94(A)
Gold Rush, panning for gold in the Dakotas, 31(A)
Gone With the Wind, premiere, 95(B)
Goodman, Benny, 93(B)
Gorbachev, Mikhail, 126(C) *Dennis Paquin*
Gorman, Margaret, 81(B)
Grable, Betty, 97(A)
Graham, Martha, 107(A) *Barbara Morgan*
Grant, Ulysses S., 39(A) *Mathew Brady*
Grant, Ulysses S. with Lee, 40(A)

Grasshoppers plague the Midwest, 92(B)
Great Train Robbery, 66(A)
Griffith, D.W., 74(A)
Groves, Leslie R., 104(B)
Guadalcanal landing, 100(A)
Guthrie, Woody, 97(A)

Hale, Nathan, 19(A) *F.O. Darley*
Harvard College, 10(A)
Hatfield family, 62(A) *T.F. Hunt*
Hayes, George E.C., 114(B)
Hemingway, Ernest, 97(A)
Hennepin, Louis, 10(A)
Henry, Patrick, 17(A)
Hindenburg, 94(B)
Hiroshima, 104(A)
Holmes, Oliver Wendell, Jr., 81(A)
Homestead Strike, 57(A)
Hoover, Herbert, 84(B)
Houdini, Harry, 68(A)
Hudson, Henry, 8(A)
Hughes, Howard, 93(B)

Irving, Washington, 28(A)
Iwo Jima, 102(B) *Joe Rosenthal*

Jackson, "Shoeless" Joe, 80(A)
Jackson, Andrew, 27(A)
Jackson, Thomas "Stonewall," 36(A) *H.A. Ogden*
James, Jesse, 41(A)
Japanese-Americans interred, 99(B)
Japanese surrender, 105(B)
Jefferson, Thomas, 22(A) *Charles Willson Peale*
Jeffries, Jim, 69(B)
Johnson, Earvin "Magic," 128(C) *Sue Ogrocki*
Johnson, Jack, 69(B)
Johnson, Lyndon B., 116(B)
Johnson, Lyndon B., signs Civil Rights Act 116(B)
Johnstown Flood, 54(A)
Jolson, Al, 84(A)
Jones, Bobby, 87(A)
Jordan, Michael, 128(C) *Sue Ogrocki*

Keller, Helen, 66(B)
Kennedy, John F. and Jacqueline Kennedy, 116(B)
Kennedy, John F. and Richard M. Nixon, 115(B)
Kennedy, Robert F., 119(B)
Kent State protest, 123(B)
Key, Francis Scott, 27(A)
King, Rev. Martin Luther, Jr., 117(B)
Kitty Hawk, the first flight, 66(A)
Korea, GI buries head in hands, 109(B)

Korea, Inchon, 109(B)
Krupa, Gene, 93(B)
Ku Klux Klan parade, 83(B)

Lafayette Escadrille, 75(B)
Lafayette, Marquis de, 19(A)
Lake Erie, Battle of, 26(A) *Percy Moran*
La Salle, René Robert Cavelier, sieur de, 9(A)
Last shot of WWI, 77(A)
Lawrence, Gertrude, 110(A)
Lee, Robert E. with Grant, 40(A)
Lennon, John, vigil, 124(B)
Leopold Jr., Nathan, 82(B)
Lewis, Meriwether, 25(I) *N.C. Wyeth*
Lincoln, Abraham, 35(A)
Lincoln, Abraham, 37(A) *Alexander Gardner*
Lincoln-Douglas Debates, 35(A)
Lincoln, Abraham, assassination of, 41(A)
Lindbergh, Charles A., 85(A)
Liston, Sonny, 118(B)
Little Big Horn, battle map, 46(A)
Little Big Horn massacre, 46(B)
Loeb, Richard, 82(B)
London, Jack, 73(B)
Louis, Joe, 95(A)
Lusitania, 74(B)
Lynching, 90(B)

MacArthur, Douglas, 103(A)
Madonna, 128(C) *Lee Celano*
Maine, the, 60(A)
Malcolm X, 117(B)
Marciano, Rocky, 112(B)
Marquette, Father Jacques, 9(A)
Marshall, Thurgood, 114(B)
Massachusetts Treasury note, 15(D)
Mather, Cotton, 12(A) *Peter Pelham*
Mays, Willie, 118(B)
McCarthy, Joseph R., 111(B)
McClellan, George, 37(A)
Mead, Margaret, 86(B)
Melville, Herman, 42(A)
Mexican War, 30(A)
Michelson, Albert A., 68(A)
Midway, Battle of, 100(B)
Migrant family, 92(A) *Dorothea Lange*
Miller, Glenn, 97(A)
Minuit, Peter, 8(A)
Minutemen at Concord Bridge, 16(A)
Mississippi steamboat, 49(A) *Currier and Ives*
Monitor vs *Merrimac*, 36(A)
Monroe, James, 28(A) *Alonzo Chappell*
Monroe, Marilyn, 113(A)
Morgan, J.P., 57(A) *Edward Steichen*
Morse, Samuel F.B., 30(B)
Morton, Dr. William T.G., 31(A)
Muir, John, 68(A)
Murrow, Edward R., 99(B)

Nabrit, James, Jr., 114(B)
National Guard in Little Rock, 114(B)
National Guard in Memphis, 114(B)
Nevada atomic testing, 111(B)
New citizens sworn in, 127(B) *Tom Salyer*
Newport, Rhode Island, 57(A)
New York Stock Exchange 1792, 24(A)
New York World's Fair, 1939, 95(A)
Nixon, Richard M., 115(B)
Nixon, Richard M. in China, 123(B)

Nixon, Richard M. resignation, 123(B)
Normandy Beach, D-Day, 101(A)

O'Neill, Eugene, 91(B)
Oakley, Annie, 53(A)
Oglethorpe, James, 12(A)
Oil Fields, Signal Hill, 87(B)
Oklahoma Land Rush, 56(A)
Olympic Hockey, 1980, 124(B)
Oppenheimer, J. Robert, 104(B)
"Over There" by George M. Cohan, 75(A)
Owens, Jesse, 93(A)

Paris, WWII liberation parade, 102(B)
Parker, Bonnie and Clyde Barrow, 91(B)
Parks, Rosa, 114(B)
Patton, George, 102(A)
Pearl Harbor, 98(B)
Pearl Harbor attack, headline, 98(B)
Peary, Robert Edwin, 69(A)
Penn, William, 8(A) *Currier and Ives*
Perry, Oliver Hazard, 26(A) *Percy Moran*
Persian Gulf, Kimberly Cano of the U.S. army, 129(C) *Pat Benic*
Persian Gulf, Marines play volleyball 129(C) *Santiago Lyon*
Persian Gulf, U.S. 82nd Airborne Division arrives, 129(B) *Martin Jeong*
Persian Gulf, U.S. Marine John Clark, 129(C) *Andy Clark*
Persian Gulf War, New York City victory parade, 130(B) *Jon Simon*
Pickett's charge, Battle of Gettysburg, 38(A)
Pickford, Mary, 81(A)
Pike's Peak, 31(A)
Pilgrim Fathers, 6(A)
Pitcher, Molly, 20(D)
Pittsburgh smokestacks, 55(A)
Pocahontas and John Rolfe, 6(A)
Poe, Edgar Allan, 28(A)
Police Station Lodgers, 54(B) *Jacob Riis*
Pony Express, 34(A)
Porter, Cole, 90(A)
Powell, John Wesley, 42(A)
Presley, Elvis, 112(B)

Reagan, Ronald, 126(C) *Dennis Paquin*
Retton, Mary Lou, 124(B)
Revere, Paul, 15(A)
Richmond, ruins of, 40(A)
Rickenbacker, Eddie, 75(A)
Robinson, Jackie, 106(A)

Rockefeller Sr., John D. and John D. Rock-efeller Jr., 74(A)
Rockne, Knute, 70(B)
Rockwell, Norman, 108(A)
Rogers, Ginger and Fred Astaire, 91(B)
Rogers, Will, 87(A)
Rolfe, John and Pocahontas, 6(A)
Roosevelt, Eleanor, 100(B)
Roosevelt, Franklin Delano, 92(B)
Roosevelt, Franklin Delano, 103(A)
Roosevelt, Theodore, 60(A)
Roosevelt, Theodore and John Muir, 68(A)
Rose, Pete, 127(B) *Terry Bochatey*
Ross, Betsy, 19(A)
Ruth, George Herman "Babe", 108(A) *Nat Fein*

Sacajawea, 25(I) *N.C. Wyeth*
Sacco, Nicola, 85(B)
Sadat, Anwar el-, 126(B) *Tim Murphy*
Salem Witch Trials, 9(A) *Howard Pyle*
Salk, Dr. Jonas, 113(B)
Sandburg, Carl, 112(B)
San Francisco Earthquake, 67(A)
Sanger, Margaret, 73(B)
San Juan Hill, Battle of, 61(A)
Schmeling, Max and Joe Louis, 95(A)
Schwarzkopf, H. Norman, 130(B) *Cliff Owen*
Segregation, 106(A)
Serapis vs. *Bonhomme Richard* 20(E) *James Hamilton*
Shockley, William, 107(B)
Sinatra, Frank, 108(B)
Sinclair, Harry F., 82(B)
Sitting Bull and Buffalo Bill Cody, 50(A)
Sousa, John Philip, 58(B)
Springsteen, Bruce, 125(A) *Doug Mills*
St. Valentine's Day Massacre, 86(B)
Stalin, Joseph, 103(A)
Standard Oil Filling Station, first, 71(A)
Star Spangled Banner, 27(A)
Statue of Liberty, 48(A)
Stengel, Casey, 115(A)
Stock Market Crash of 1929, 88(B)
Stuart, James Ewell Brown "Jeb," 38(A)
Suffragette parade, 72(A)
Super Bowl I, 118(B)

Tarring and feathering, 15(D)
Teapot Dome scandal, 82(B)

Tea Act, New York City broadside, 14(D)
Television, 84(B)
Temple, Shirley, 91(A)
Thanksgiving, first, 7(A)
The King and I, 110(A)
The Spirit of '76, 17(J) *Archibald M. Willard*
The Wizard of Oz, 95(A)
Thomas, Clarence, 130(C)
Thorpe, Jim, 70(B)
Tilden, Bill, 82(B)
Tippecanoe, Battle of, 26(A) *Kurz and Allison*
Titanic, 73(B) *Willy Stoewer*
Tory drummed out of colonial village, 15(A) *C.S. Reinhart*
Transcontinental railroad, 43(A)
Truman, Harry S., 108(B)
Truth, Sojourner, 32(A)
Tunney, Gene and Jack Dempsey, 84(A)
Twain, Mark, 52(A)

U.S.S. Missouri, 104(B)
Uncle Tom's Cabin 33(A)
Underground Railroad placard, 32(A)
Union Army in combat, 39(A) *Timothy O'Sullivan*

V-J Day, 104(B)
Valentino, Rudolph 84(B)
Valley Forge, 19(A) *Alonzo Chappell*
Vanzetti, Bartolomeo, 85(B)
Verrazano, Giovanni da, 4(A)
Versailles Peace Conference, 78(A)
Vespucci, Amerigo, 2(A)
Veteran, black, wounded, WWI, 78(B)
Viet Cong booby trap, 120(B) *Nguyen Thanh Tai*
Vietnam, "Dream of a Better Life", 120(B) *Toshio Sakai*
Vietnam, Americans escape, 121(B)
Vietnam, U.S. 101st Airborne Brigade, 120(B)
Vietnam, U.S. first Air Cavalry Division, 121(B) *Jeff Taylor*
Vietnam, USAF Captain Michael S. Kerr returns home, 121(B)
Vietnam Veterans Memorial, 125(B)
Virginia advertisement for colonists, 6(A)

Wall Street during 1857 panic, 34(A) *Cafferty and Rosenberg*
Washington, George, 22(A) *Gilbert Stuart*
Washington, George crossing the Dela-ware, 18(A) *Emanuel Leutze*
Watson, Dr. James Dewey, 115(B)
Webster, Noah, 25(A) *Root and Tinker*
Weicker, Lowell, 123(B)
Weissmuller, Johnny, 86(A)
Welles, Orson, 96(A)
Whitman, Walt, 47(A)
Whitney, Eli, 24(A)
Wilson, Woodrow, 78(A)
Woman factory worker, WWII, 101(A)
Woodhull, Victoria, 44(A)
Wounded Knee massacre, 58(A)
Wright, Frank Lloyd, 112(B)
Wright, Orville and Wilbur, 66(A)

Yeltsin, Boris, 128(B) *Joe Marquette*
Yorktown, Cornwallis's surrender, 20(E) *John Trumbull*

Key to Picture Sources

(A) The Bettman Archive
(B) Bettman/UPI
(C) Reuter/Bettman
(D) Dover Publications
(E) Yale University Art Gallery
(F) Virginia University of Fine Arts
(G) The Metropolitan Museum of Art
(H) Washington University Gallery of Art, St. Louis
(I) Brunnier Gallery and Museum, Iowa State University
(J) Abbot Hall, Marblehead, Massachusetts

Endpaper art courtesy of Yale University Art Gallery